THE
NEW BOOK
OF THE
HORSE

THE

NEW BOOK
OF THE
HORSE

HOWELL
BOOK HOUSE

Maxwell Macmillan International
TORONTO

Maxwell Macmillan International
NEW YORK OXFORD SINGAPORE SYDNEY

A QUARTO BOOK

Copyright © 1990 by Quarto Publishing plc

First American Edition, 1990

Howell Book House
Macmillan Publishing Company
866 Third Avenue, New York, NY 10022

Maxwell Macmillan Canada, Inc.
1200 Eglinton Avenue East
Suite 200
Don Mills, Ontario M3C 3N1

Library of Congress Cataloging-in-Publication Data

Haw, Sarah.
    The new book of the horse / Sarah Haw. — 1st American ed.
        p.   cm.
    ISBN 0-87605-883-7
    1. Horsemanship.   2. Horses.   3. Horse sports.   1. Title.

SF309.H388 1990   89-29031 CIP
798.2–dc20

Macmillan books are available at special discounts for bulk purchases for sales
promotions, premiums, fund-raising, or educational use. For details contact:

Special Sales Director
Macmillan Publishing Company
866 Third Avenue
New York, NY 10022

This book was designed and produced by
Quarto Publishing plc
The Old Brewery
6 Blundell Street
London N7 9BH

Senior Editor   Cathy Meeus
Project Editor   Helen Douglas-Cooper

Designer   Hazel Edington

Photographer   Bob Langrish

Illustrator   Jim Robins

Art Director   Nick Buzzard

Quarto would also like to thank the following for their help in the preparation of
this book: Gillian Cooper, David Kemp.

10 9 8 7 6 5 4 3 2

Typeset in Great Britain by Ampersand Typesetting (Bournemouth) Ltd
Manufactured in Hong Kong by Regent Publishing Services Ltd
Printed in Hong Kong by Leefung Asco Printers Ltd

CONTENTS

SECTION

1

THE HORSE

12 Breeding and rearing
14 How horses are bred
16 The birth of a foal
18 Handling a foal
20 Mares and foals
22 Learning to lead
24 Tying up
25 Weaning
26 Breaking in

28 Owning a Horse
30 A horse of your own
34 What type of horse: general riding
36 What type of horse: show jumping
38 What type of horse: dressage
40 What type of horse: eventing
42 Where to buy
44 Stabling at home
46 Stabling: boarding out
48 Stabling: part-board
50 Stable routine
52 Grooming
54 Feeding
56 Tack and clothing
58 Health

SECTION

2

HORSE AND RIDER

64 Riding Techniques
66 The rider's position
70 The aids
72 The walk
74 The trot
76 The canter
78 Upward transitions
80 Downward transitions
82 Turns and circles
84 Improver lesson: sluggish horses
86 Improver lesson: fizzy horses
88 Artificial aids
90 The jumping position
92 Pole work
94 Poles leading to a small jump
96 Individual fences
98 Jumping doubles

100 Leisure Riding
102 Trail riding: 1
104 Trail riding: 2

SECTION

3

COMPETITIVE RIDING

110 Show-Jumping
112 Correct equipment
114 Pole work
116 Grid work
118 Uprights
120 Spreads
122 Combination fences
126 Spooky fences
132 Riding a course

140 Dressage
142 Clothing and tack
144 Dressage training
146 The walk
148 The trot
152 The canter
154 Transitions
158 Turn on the forehand
159 Counter canter
160 Shoulder-in
162 The half-pass
164 Leg yielding
165 Walk pirouette
166 Passage and piaffe
167 Riding a dressage test

168 Eventing
170 Safety equipment
172 The cross-country position
174 Gridwork
180 Cross-country fences
182 Bounce fences
184 Corner fences
186 Table fences
188 Drop fences
190 Downhill fences
192 Uphill fences
194 Steps
198 Water fences

200 Glossary
204 Index

SECTION

THE HORSE

BREEDING AND REARING
·
OWNING A HORSE

Horse-riding stands apart from other sports because of one key element – the horse. At every level of riding, from the one-horse owner content to ride out for pleasure, to the professional competitive rider, the relationship with the horse is paramount and fundamental.

We tend to think of the horse as a domesticated animal, but the instincts of the wild horse can be recognized in the behavior of the modern horse. Horses are gregarious creatures; they lived together in large herds for friendship and mutual protection. The modern horse is always happier in the company of other horses. In the wild, if a horse felt threatened it would either flee or fight back by kicking, bucking and biting. If a horse is frightened or taken by surprise by features of the modern world it will

The Arab

The Arab is one of the oldest and most beautiful breeds in the world. It epitomizes the strength, speed and spirit of the horse that have made it the object of man's admiration and affection over the centuries.

react in the same way. And if it feels uncomfortable or unbalanced because, for example, it is too constrained by its rider, it will fight the constraint or try to run away from the cause of the discomfort.

It is important that you understand these instincts if you are to build a good relationship with your horse.

Strength and daring (right)

Horses have great courage, and when teamed with a good horseman or horsewoman, are capable of feats of considerable athleticism and daring, as demonstrated by Ginny Leng on Master Craftsman.

Complete harmony (left)

The close co-operation and understanding that can develop between horse and man reaches its fullest expression in the art of dressage.

Companionship (above)

Horses were originally herd animals, and they are always happier in the company of other horses.

BREEDING AND REARING

The relationship between horse and human begins as soon as the foal is born. The foal should become used to the presence and attentions of its handler as early as possible. It should be taught to wear a foal slip, lead with its mother, and stay tied up quietly while it is still quite young, and through these lessons it should learn to trust and obey its handler. Every lesson should be taken gradually, step by step, and nothing should be rushed. Only when you are quite confident that the youngster is happy and confident, and knows exactly what is expected of it, should you progress on to the next stage.

In this section we look at the early handling and training of a foal, and the way in which this creates the basis for a fruitful and co-operative relationship between horse and human.

Hanoverian stallions

The Hanoverian has always been popular for dressage and show-jumping. It also produces excellent horses for these disciplines when crossed with lighter breeds such as the Thoroughbred.

Lunging (above)

Lunging is a vital part of the training of a young horse. It is also useful for schooling and exercising older horses.

Rocky Mountain pony (left)

The USA does not have any indigenous breeds. However, pony breeds such as the Rocky mountain pony, have been developed by crossing native horse breeds with pony stock imported from countries such as the UK. American horse breeds include the Morgan, the American Saddlebred, the Standardbred and the Tennessee Walking horse.

How horses are bred

When considering whether to breed a mare, you must be honest about whether she measures up in terms of temperament, conformation, soundness and action. In addition, a bad-tempered mare will pass this on to her foal, whereas foals of good-tempered mares tend to be trusting and friendly.

The choice of stallion for a mare is all important, and there are two main aspects that you should consider. Firstly, study his bloodlines, as you want a stallion that will pass on his good qualities. Secondly, study the stallion himself. You should look for good conformation, action and temperament, soundness, performance, and a good constitution.

Most mares come into season or "heat" for approximately five days every three weeks for three or four months during spring and summer each year. It is during this time that the mare will be 'served' or 'covered' by the stallion. As pregnancy lasts for about eleven months, the foal will be born when the weather is at its kindest and there is plenty of grass.

However, the demands of today's competitive world dictate that some horses need to be bred much earlier in the year.

Racehorses, for instance, need to mature as early as possible if they are to race as two-year-olds, and top-class show horses need to look their best when shown as young stock. Such are the advances in veterinary science that many top brood mares have their estrus cycle changed to enable them to have early foals.

The most natural way of having a mare covered is to turn her out and let her run with the stallion. He will soon learn to tell when the mare is receptive. However, as

stallions can command high fees and their progeny large sums of money at the sales, the natural method can be a little risky. In such cases, covering is carefully controlled. Mares are sent to the breeding farm around five days before they come into season and will stay there for six to nine weeks.

The breeding manager will watch the mare for signs that she is coming into season, and she will be tried either by the stallion or by a teaser. Once it is established that she is in season, the covering will take place.

Sociability (above)

A large herd of mares and foals grazing peacefully together. Horses are sociable animals who enjoy companionship.

The Irish National Stud (left)

At this Thoroughbred farm, high-class stallions stand at reasonable fees, and small breeders can bring their mares here for foaling. It is also an important center for research into subjects related to reproduction and feeding.

A large Australian stud (above)

Mares and foals at the Imperial Stud, New South Wales, Australia.

Lippizaner mares and foals (below)

The Lippizaners have been made famous by the Spanish Riding School of Vienna, whose displays of high-school dressage are popular throughout the world.

Covering

The mare's tail is bandaged and her feet fitted with felt boots to minimize damage to the stallion should she kick. Several breeding assistants are needed to make sure that all goes well.

However, with an experienced stallion and mare, there should not be any problems. The covering itself takes about two minutes.

The birth of a foal

Pregnancy lasts for about eleven months, although it can vary by a few days, or even weeks, with a first foal.

There are several signs that foaling is near. The udder becomes swollen (known as 'bagging up'), the teats become waxy, the muscles around the hindquarters slacken and the shape of the mare changes as the foal 'drops' ready for birth.

Major breeding farms employ closed-circuit television and round-the-clock supervision for their charges, which foal in specially prepared, large foaling boxes. As the majority of mares foal in the quiet of the night, many amateur owners never see the event. This should not be cause for concern, however, as most births run smoothly.

Most mares lie down once foaling begins. The foal's forelegs should appear first, wrapped in the amnion (the whitish/yellow bag which contains the amniotic fluid). The mare should be allowed to get on with foaling on her own unless she is obviously having difficulties. Foals should be born in the diving position with their heads tucked between their forelegs. However, there can

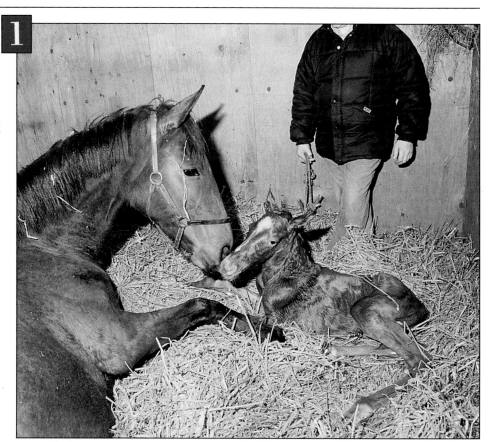

be problems: a leg may be bent, the head may be twisted back, or a breech birth (when the hindlegs appear first) may occur. If there seems to be any problem with the positioning of the foal, or if the mare is straining excessively or getting up and down, expert help will be needed.

Most foals will stand up and search for milk within about half an hour of birth. The umbilical cord should break of its own accord, and simply needs to be dabbed with a little antiseptic powder.

The placenta should come away from the mare too and needs to be kept carefully for checking by the vet. If any part of it is left inside the mare it can cause infection.

With a first foal, the mare's udder may be sore and ticklish, and she may need some encouragement to allow the foal to suckle. Suckling is a vital part of the process. As well as helping the bonding process between mare and foal, it provides the foal with colostrum, the first milk flow, which contains important antibodies. It also helps in the process of passing the meconium, the first droppings.

Foaling

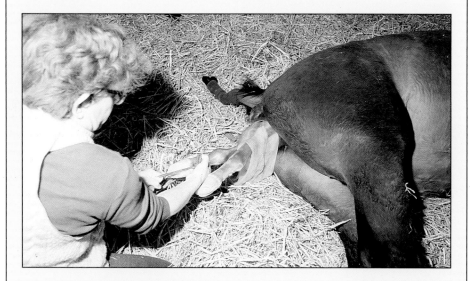

Most mares lie down to foal. Foals should be born in the diving position, with their forelegs appearing first. The mare should be left to get on with foaling on her own, unless she is having problems. Only an experienced person should assist in the process.

The newborn foal

1 Immediately after birth the mare cleans and nuzzles her foal, and encourages it to try to stand up.

2 Most foals will be on their feet and searching for milk within about half an hour of foaling.

3 Twenty-four hours later: a healthy foal and a contented mother.

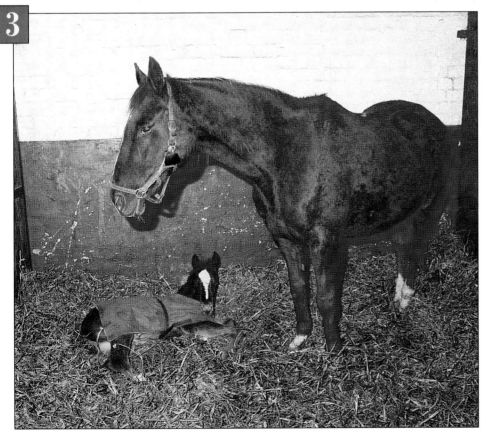

Handling a foal

The basis of a good relationship between human and horse is trust, and this should be developed from the very beginning. The sooner a young foal learns to accept the attentions and instructions of its handler, the better.

Foals are usually stabled with their mothers after birth, and then progress to short periods in the field, eventually being turned out for most of the day and coming in at night. While the foal is in the stable the handler can accustom it to human attention by spending some minutes morning and evening talking to it, petting it and running his or her hands over its neck, back and legs. The foal will not take long to realize that no harm is intended, and the beginnings of a good relationship will be established.

One of the early lessons that should be taught to a foal is to have a foal slip fitted, and this can be done as early as a couple of days after birth. A foal slip is a miniature version of a halter, and can be fitted in the stable.

Three people are needed. One stands on the foal's near side and places the left arm around the foal's chest, the right one around its hindquarters and tail. The foal is held firmly and securely and the second person carefully puts the foal slip on the foal, ensuring that it fits comfortably so that the foal does not associate the fitting with discomfort or pain. However, it should be fitted tight enough to prevent the foal getting its foot caught if it scratches its head.

The third person holds the mare. The foal slip should be taken off when the foal comes in to the stable at night.

Wearing a foal slip

A foal should wear a foal slip from an early age as this will make handling and leading much easier.

A healthy foal (above)

A mare and her young foal enjoy the freedom of being turned out for the summer.

Charming vulnerability (right)

A Welsh pony foal, one of the prettiest and most elegant of the pony breeds.

Mares and foals

Soon after foaling, mare and foal should be turned out on good pasture for the summer. Thoroughbred mares and foals should be turned out each day in good weather, but brought in at night. Other breeds can stay out at night as long as the weather is mild. Great care must be paid to their nutrition as lactation makes great demands on the mare, and the foal needs to grow strong and healthy. In the case of Thoroughbreds, high quality hard feed should be fed when they are brought in to the stable.

Even foals that live out all the time are best caught up and brought in with the mare each day for a grooming and handling session, so that the vital link between foal and trainer can be established.

Exmoor mare and foal (above)

The Exmoor is the oldest of the British native breeds. It is exceptionally hardy and strong, and at the same time is agile and intelligent. Exmoors have been exported all over the world to be used as foundation stock as, crossed with Thoroughbred bloodlines, they produce excellent stock.

The first summer (left)

Mare and foal should be turned out on good quality pasture, so that the foal is given the best possible start.

Arab mare and foal (above)

The Arab is now bred all over the world. It is the oldest and most influential pure breed. As well as being used for riding, it is also widely used for improving other breeds.

Standardbred foals (below)

Companionship is important for young foals and will help them through the difficult process of weaning.

Learning to lead

This is a lesson which should be taught as early as possible, ideally as soon as the mare and foal start to go out in the field.

A helper stands at the foal's near shoulder and passes a soft piece of cloth, such as a stable rubber, around its neck and holds it with the left hand while placing the right hand around the foal's quarters. Following the mare, the foal can be encouraged forwards by pushing on its hindquarters and using an appropriate phrase like 'walk on'.

The foal should never be pulled along but, as it relaxes with each repeated lesson, the pressure on the hindquarters can be lessened, until it leads quite happily off the stable rubber.

Once the handler is satisfied that the foal is relaxed and knows what is expected of it, he can progress to leading it off the foal slip.

Even in the early stages, the handler's voice is very important, to encourage and praise. Verbal commands can be learned quite easily by the foal and will stay with it right through its life.

Handling legs and feet

The early learning process should include teaching a foal to have its feet and legs handled. A foal's feet will need regular trimming from the age of about two months and by preparing the youngster for the farrier, you will make this easier for it to cope with.

Start by handling the legs and feet as part of the overall handling process. Then get the foal used to having its feet picked up. Push it gently sideways so that it shifts its weight over, and pick up its foot at the same time, saying "up", and it will soon understand what is required.

Once the foal is used to having its feet picked up, accustom it to having them picked out and tap the pick on its foot so that it realizes it will not be harmed. Again, make much of any successes.

Leading (top)

The sooner a foal is taught to be led, the better. Quite quickly it should be happy to be led by the handler with its mother.

A well-behaved foal (above)

This young foal is growing on well. It is relaxed and standing quietly with its handler.

The maternal instinct (left)

A mare shelters her young foal from the wind.

Herd instinct (below)

These foals show early signs of the herd instinct as they nuzzle and groom each other.

Tying up

A young foal must learn to be tied up and left on its own, and this lesson should be taught with patience and care. It should be taught in a stable with plenty of bedding on the floor so that the foal is unlikely to slip. Do not tie up a youngster properly until you are certain that it will not panic, and always tie it up using a quick release knot attached to a breakable piece of string because a youngster can easily damage its neck by pulling back on its halter. You should always stay nearby until you are sure that it will remain quietly on its own. Leave the foal tied up for increasingly longer periods of time, until it will stay quietly tied up for about an hour.

Learning to tie up

1 The lesson is taught in the stable. The foal has a lunge line attached to its halter, and the lunge line is passed through a tying-up ring, with the handler holding the other end.

2 The foal will probably fight against the restriction of the lunge line at first, but with the handler holding the other end, it should not come to any harm.

3 Once the foal accepts being tied up, the handler makes a fuss of it so that it understands that this behaviour is appreciated.

Weaning

Weaning, the separation of the foal from the mare, should be completed by six months of age. If the foal continues suckling after this time, it is likely to weaken the mare and make her anemic.

There are several schools of thought on the best way to wean.

One method is to stable mare and foal together for a few days, and then to remove the mare beyond ear-shot.

On the other hand, some people are in favour of keeping the mare within calling distance of a foal, so that the foal is comforted by the sounds of the mare after they have been separated.

Either way, the foal is kept stabled for several days, and is then best turned out with other youngsters so that it has company.

Another method is to turn a group of mares and foals out together, and gradually remove the mares until only the youngsters remain.

It will now be autumn, and the foal should be kept in at night and be out during the day. When the warm summer weather returns, it can be kept out all the time. The youngster's life follows this pattern for the next couple of years, during which time it should be allowed to grow on and enjoy itself.

Weaning the foal (above)

Weaning can be a traumatic experience for a youngster, and it needs to be handled with tact and common sense.

Mustang foals (left)

A group of mustang youngsters running together. Youngsters should be allowed to grow on until their third year, when breaking and training begin.

Breaking in

Most horses are broken in at three years old. The exceptions are racehorses, which may be racing at two years old, and certain other breeds which mature early.

'Breaking in' is an inappropriate term for a process that demands great patience, sensitivity and understanding. To the uninitiated, it may look as if a horse is left untouched until, at three, it is suddenly taught to obey the commands of a trainer and have a rider on its back. However, if the education of the horse started right from its earliest days, the basic principles of communication and co-operation will have been laid down already, and 'breaking in' is just an extension and development of these. The horse will already know how to obey the instructions of its trainer, it will respect and trust him or her, and it will know that obedience brings reward.

Once the horse has learned to be led in hand, breaking in begins with lunging. To

begin with a helper leads the horse around until it understands what is expected of it. The trainer stands in the center of the circle that the horse is working on, forming a triangle with lunge-rein, whip and horse. The trainer uses the voice, backed up by the lunge whip to give commands.

The next stage is to fit a roller, with a breastplate to prevent it slipping back, to simulate the feel of a girth, and this is later replaced by a saddle.

The first fitting of a bit is done using a mouthing bit. This is left in for short periods to accustom the horse to it, and again when the horse is worked on the lunge.

The feel of the reins can be introduced by using long-reins or side-reins.

Finally, the rider is introduced to the horse by backing, the beginning of a process which, if all goes well, will see the horse develop into an obedient, forward-going ride.

Lunging

Once the horse has become accustomed to wearing a saddle, it is lunged with the saddle in place.

Long-reining (left)

Long-reins pass either side of the horse from the bit to the handler, who walks behind. They accustom the horse to the feel of the reins.

Side-reins (right)

Side-reins attach to the bit and the girth straps on the saddle. Again, they accustom the horse to the feel of the reins, and can be used when the horse is being lunged.

Backing (left)

To begin with the rider just leans across the horse's back. Eventually she swings her leg over and sits up in the saddle.

OWNING A HORSE

When you are deciding whether to buy a horse of your own, you have to make many different choices. Firstly you have to decide what type of horse will suit your requirements and your own ability. You have to decide how and where to keep it. This, again, will depend on what type of riding you want to do and whether you will be entering competitions regularly, as a stabled horse can be kept much fitter than a pastured horse, which will not be fit enough for much more than general riding. You will need to decide whether you have the facilities and time to keep the horse at home, or whether you will need to keep it at a boarding stable, bearing in mind that

if you look after the horse yourself you will be able to develop a much better relationship.

Good general management and sensitive care of a horse does much to maximize a horse's potential, as a horse that is correctly fed, comfortable and relaxed will be fit, willing, and contented in its work.

Exercising

If you are keeping a stabled horse, you must have the time to exercise it each day as well as for all the management and stable duties.

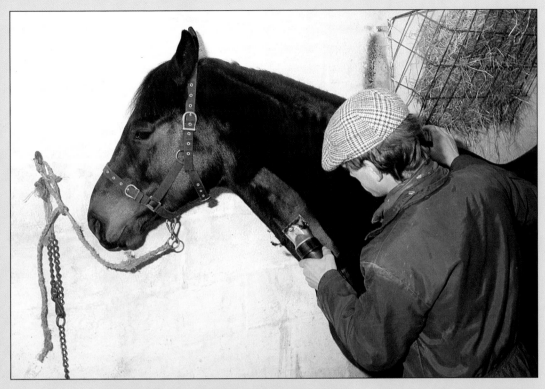

Ownership (left)

Owning a horse is a great responsibility, and looking after a stabled horse is almost a full-time activity.

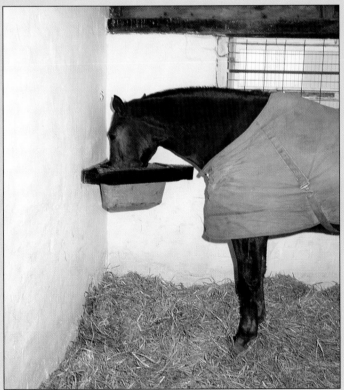

Good care (above)

If your horse is well cared for, comfortable and correctly fed, you will be able to get the maximum performance out of it.

Making a choice (right)

Look for a horse that has ability and the willingness to co-operate with you whatever type of riding you intend to participate in.

A horse of your own: 1

Once you have been taking riding lessons for a while, and you have read as much as you can about owning a horse, sit down and think it through carefully before making a final decision. Make a list of the pros and cons, and talk it over with your family and friends before you finally decide to go ahead. And once you have decided to buy a horse, you need to think about what sort of horse to get to suit what you want to do; and what will be the most convenient way for you to keep it.

Take a long, hard look at your riding ability and horse-management know-how. It is one thing to go riding once a week at the local riding school, but quite another to go out on your own and deal with a nervous horse in a tricky situation. If you know that your riding is quite good, but you doubt that you would be able, or willing, to handle a horse without some back-up, take this into account when thinking about the type of horse you should look for and where you should keep it.

The same applies to looking after a horse. It is one thing to know what to do when there are knowledgeable people around to support you, quite another when you are on your own.

Owning a horse is a big commitment, and it will take up a lot of your time. Horses need a routine that is kept to as closely as possible seven days a week. They need feeding and watering, mucking out and grooming. A single horse will thrive from your company, and a horse that is stabled will need even more attention than one which is out at pasture.

Hosing down

Looking after a horse is not all hard work: horses and riders enjoy cooling off in the heat at Palm Beach.

Making friends (below)

You will need to spend plenty of time with your horse, getting to know it and establishing a good rapport.

Road exercise (above)

Regular road exercise is a vital part of getting a horse fit.

Mucking out (right)

Once of the many jobs that have to be done daily if you have your own horse.

A horse of your own: 2

When you are considering whether to buy a horse, you must take into account the cost of the whole enterprise, which involves much more than the cost of the horse itself.

Firstly there is the horse's accommodation, whether it is in a supervised boarding stable where everything is done for you, down the road in a local farmer's field, or whether you are going to convert a building on your own land.

Next there is the tack and equipment. This includes not just the saddle and bridle, but items like a halter, grooming kit, first aid kit and blankets. If you are keeping the horse yourself rather than at livery you will also need to include the costs of mucking out gear, feed bins, buckets and haynets.

Unless feed is included in the board bill, you need to calculate the costs of concentrate feed, hay and any supplements.

The horse will need to be shod, or at the least have its feet trimmed, every six to eight weeks, be wormed every two months, and have its teeth rasped twice a year. The horse will have to be insured. And you will need

Riding out (above)

One of the pleasures of owning your own horse lies in being able to ride out with friends.

Washing down at a show (left)

Many people enjoy the fun and the challenge of competitive riding.

to allow for extra funds to cover the vet's bills in the case of an accident.

Do you have all the right clothing for yourself? Apart from the basics such as an approved hard hat or crash hat, jodhpurs and boots, you may want to compete with your horse. You need to take into account the cost of a show jacket or cross-country gear, depending on what you want to do, together with the additional safety equipment needed for your horse.

If you want to enter competitions you will need to take into account entrance fees, the cost of transporting the horse and of protective equipment for traveling.

You should also include the cost of having lessons on your own horse. This will be invaluable in ironing out any problems you have and in preparing you for any shows or competitive events that you want to enter.

Finally, when buying the horse, remember to allow for the cost of having it checked over by a vet, and for traveling it home.

Riding activities (above)

As well as the main areas of show-jumping, dressage and eventing, there are other competitive fields that you can enter, such as endurance riding.

Exercising (left)

Your horse will need to be exercised every day whatever the weather conditions.

What type of horse: general riding

When looking for a horse, the first thing you must remember is that the perfect horse does not exist. Although you should obviously not buy a horse thinking that you can correct all its faults, you must accept that you are unlikely to find a horse that is perfect in every way.

As well as breeds and cross-breeds, there are types of horse, referring to the work for which they have been bred. For example, the terms show-jumper and eventer do not refer to a breed, or to conformation or appearance, but to their ability.

Look for good conformation, as this will indicate that the horse will be a well-balanced ride. It should have strong, well-made limbs, sloping shoulders, a strong back and hindquarters, a well set-on neck and head, and a generous eye. Overall, it should look compact and strong.

Whatever type of riding you want to do, it is very important that you choose a horse that suits your own ability and standard of riding, and one whose temperament suits your own personality. If it is your first horse, look for one that is reliable and experienced. You will not get much pleasure from riding if you fall for a young, unsuitable horse and find yourself with a mass of problems.

When you try a horse, ask yourself whether it feels right for you? Are you having to hold it back, or push it on? A timid rider on a timid horse will seldom be a successful combination, nor will a dominant rider on a sensitive horse. On the other hand, a dominant rider on a placid horse, or a timid rider on an outgoing, reliable horse will often develop a very successful relationship.

The Irish cob (above)

Ireland produces some of the best riding cobs. A good cob is an excellent general riding and show horse.

The Andalusian (right)

The Andalusian, which originates from Spain but has been exported to many parts of the world, is a very beautiful horse. In addition, it has a calm temperament and is easy to handle. It has been crossed with Arabs and Thoroughbreds to produce excellent general riding horses.

The Saddlebred (above)

The Saddlebred is one of the most elegant of the American breeds. It is excellent in the show-ring as well as being a good horse for pleasure riding.

The Appaloosa (left)

The Appaloosa is descended from sixteenth-century Spanish stock. The breed was originally developed by the Nez Perce Indians. It is courageous and easy to handle, and is popular as a pleasure and parade horse.

What type of horse: show-jumping

When buying a horse for show-jumping, look for one that is an easy ride. Do not choose a horse that is complicated to ride, however much ability it has, because it is more important that it is keen to co-operate than that it is clever. The horse should have a good, open eye and a pleasant nature.

Look for a horse that is sound and goes in a nice fashion. Look for strong hindquarters and hocks that will give it the power and thrust needed to spring out over the fences.

When you go to see a horse, take someone with you who you trust, who knows about horses, and who will give you an unbiased opinion. Watch it being ridden over fences as well as trying it yourself. Does the horse lift its front legs from the shoulders, and make a good shape over the fence? Watch it over a combination, and study its mental reaction as well as its technique. If it falters, it may be an indication of a lack of self-confidence.

English, Irish and American breeds and cross-breeds are good for show-jumping. The German breeds, such as Hanoverians, need a very strong rider, although through cross-breeding with breeds such as the Thoroughbred, they are becoming more suitable for the ordinary rider.

A talent for jumping (below)

Thomas Fruhmann on Grandeur. Every horse has a natural talent for jumping, which is improved and developed by training.

An abundance of ability (left)

John Whitaker on Next Milton at the European Championships, 1989. A show-jumper needs character and ability. This very successful and popular horse has an abundance of both.

A top-class athlete (below)

Michel Robert on Pequignet Lafayette. Many different types of horse are seen in the show-jumping ring. The one thing they all have in common is that they are top-class athletes.

Physical strength (right)

Michael Whitaker on Next Monsanta taking a large spread at Calgary, 1989. A show-jumper needs strong hindquarters and hocks, to give it the power to spring out over big fences.

What type of horse: dressage

When looking for a horse for dressage, look particularly for good paces and a good temperament. The horse should also be well made, as this produces a better balanced horse and one that will find the different types of gaits and movements easier to learn. A horse that has a very long back and a short neck, for example, will find collected work very difficult.

Look for nice gaits, with good, regular steps. The horse should move well, with freedom in the shoulders and active hocks. The walk should be free and swinging. The trot should be energetic, with elasticity in the movement and a clear moment of suspension. The canter should be light, with a clear 3-time step.

Most important of all, look for a horse with a good temperament, and which you feel you will get on with, because more than any other equestrian sport, dressage requires total harmony between horse and rider.

For a long time, German breeds were popular because of the quality of their movement. Now they have been used to improve the English and American breeds for dressage, and any type is suitable as long as it moves well and you feel that it is right for you.

Good gaits (above)

Margit Otto Crepin on Corlandus at the European Championships, 1989. Look for a horse that has good gaits and moves well.

The dressage type (left)

Dr Reiner Klimke on Ahlerich 2 at the 1988 Olympics. Many different types of horse are now used in dressage, although the current fashion is for lighter types.

Compatibility (above)

Marie Meyers on Dimitrius performing at Stockholm, 1989. Choose a horse that feels right for you.

Good conformation (right)

Cynthia Ishoy on Dynasty at the 1988 Olympics. A horse that has good conformation will find the different gaits and movements easier to learn.

What type of horse: eventing

The three disciplines of eventing – dressage, cross-country, and show-jumping – require a horse that has fluid gaits and precision of movement, speed and stamina, and good jumping ability. Being an all-rounder it need not have outstanding jumping ability, but it must be a good jumper and neat in front.

It must be physically sound, tough-looking and brave. At the same time it should have a generous eye, a good temperament, and be obedient, because it must constantly be listening and responding to its rider. Like the show-jumper it must be very strong in the hindquarters and hocks, to give it the strength to tackle difficult obstacles on all types of terrain.

Thoroughbred-type horses or Thoroughbred crosses are popular. The Thoroughbred blood provides obedience and poise, while for example hunter or pony blood provides courage, endurance, aggressiveness and cleverness.

Thoroughbred type (above)

Virginia Leng on Master Craftsman. Thoroughbred-type horses are popular for eventing.

Pony blood (right)

Madelaine Gurdon on The Done Thing. Pony blood gives an eventer courage, cleverness and endurance.

An all-rounder (above)

Mark Todd on Charisma. The event horse must be an all-rounder. As well as the toughness and jumping ability needed for the cross-country and show-jumping phases, it must have the precision of movement and fluid gaits that are looked for in the dressage test.

The eventing type (left)

Tanya Longson on Pink Fizz. No one breed makes an eventer. The horse needs ability, speed, stamina and boldness.

Where to buy

Once you have made the decision to buy a horse of your own, and you know what type you want, you have to set about finding one.

Begin by asking around locally. Contact everyone you know, ask at your local riding school, the local saddlers and feed merchants, all of whom may know of horses for sale. Go through the advertisements in the local papers and the equestrian magazines. If a good horse dealer is recommended to you, try him, but as a first-time buyer you would be well advised not to buy from horse sales.

Buying a horse is the beginning of a long-term partnership, and it is worth taking time and trouble over your choice. When you go to try a horse, take someone else with you, preferably someone who has plenty of experience.

Find out as much information as you can on the telephone before traveling to see a horse. Advertisements can be misleading, and there is little point in traveling to see a horse only to find on arrival that it is totally unsuitable.

Handle the horse thoroughly when you go to try it, just as you would at home. Pick up its feet, lead it in a halter, tie it up.

Ride it yourself on the flat and over some jumps. Ask to see the horse ridden out on the road and watch its behavior carefully, particularly with traffic. Consider asking about taking it for a trial period of one or two weeks.

Make a note in advance of all the questions you want to ask so that you do not forget any of them. Do not rush into a decision about the first horse you see. And do not be afraid to say if it is not right.

Never buy a horse without having it vetted, even if it appears perfectly sound to you. Finally, be honest with yourself and buy a horse which is within your capabilities. That way, you will have much more fun with it.

Horse auctions

Auctions of any sort are daunting places to buy, and you have no way of checking in advance whether the horse is sound.

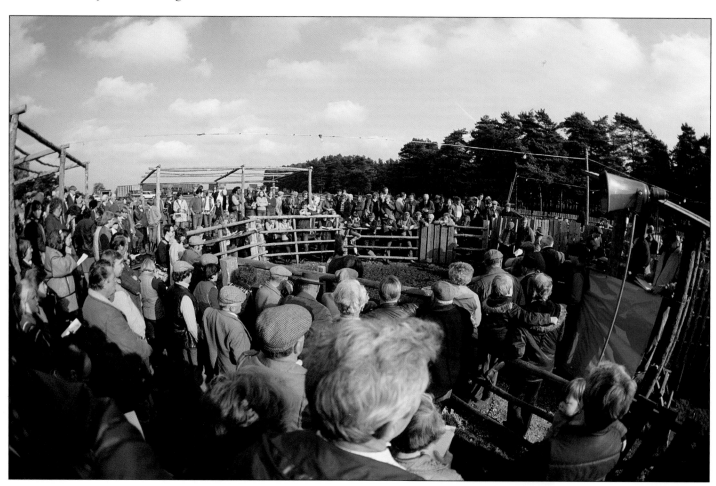

Horse sales (left)

Horse sales are fascinating to visit, but the first-time buyer would be well-advised not to buy at them.

Veterinary check (below)

Always have a horse thoroughly checked over by a vet before you commit yourself to buying it.

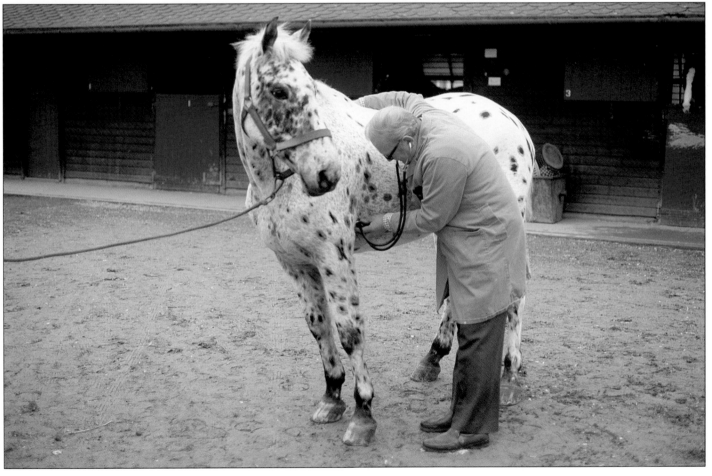

Stabling at home

Stabling at home is the ideal way of keeping a horse if you have land, suitable buildings and plenty of time.

If you are beginning from scratch, you will need to build or convert stables, plus feed storage and tack-room facilities. You will need to install water and lighting, and to have the paddock area, which needs to be a minimum of 1½ acres per horse, properly fenced off. Even if you have a very hardy horse that will live out a lot of the time, you will need a minimum of 1½ acres of land, and some form of stabling or shelter.

The loosebox or stall needs to be warm, well ventilated and draught-free. It should be large enough to allow the horse to lie down. It should also have good drainage and be vermin-proof. It should face away from prevailing winds, and have a pleasant outlook, preferably onto the stable yard or onto an area where there is plenty of activity to give the horse something to look at.

The fencing around any pasture must be strong and solid. Long-lasting materials such as wooden posts and rails are ideal, but are expensive. Posts and wire is a less expensive but equally satisfactory alternative. Gates should be strong and secure, and must swing easily. They should fasten properly without needing to be tied with string.

Bedding (below)

Straw is a good bedding material. It should be banked up around the sides of the stall to exclude draughts and help prevent the horse injuring itself at night.

Types of stabling (left)

The American system (far left), which is used at large equestrian centers, and the single loosebox (left) offer alternative methods of stabling. In the American system, there are several stalls separated off with metal bars, which make them more light and airy. Individual looseboxes take up more room, but are the obvious choice for keeping one or two horses.

Suitable fencing and gates

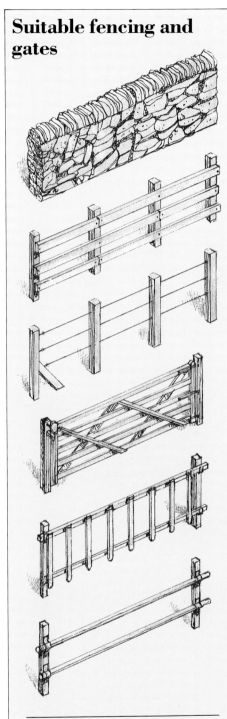

From the top: dry stone wall; post and rail post and wire; traditional five-bar wooden gate; metal gate; and slip rails.

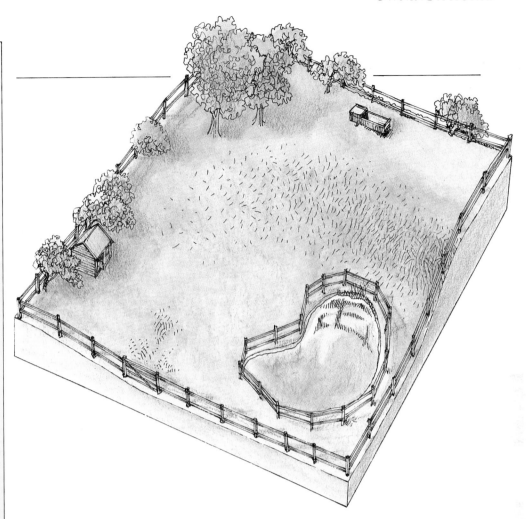

A well maintained paddock (above)

Good pasture, a sturdy gate, good fencing, a water trough with mains supply, and a field shelter. Stagnant water, such as the pond here, should be fenced off and an alternative water supply provided.

Home stabling (below)

Keeping a horse at home and looking after it yourself enables you to establish a good relationship with it.

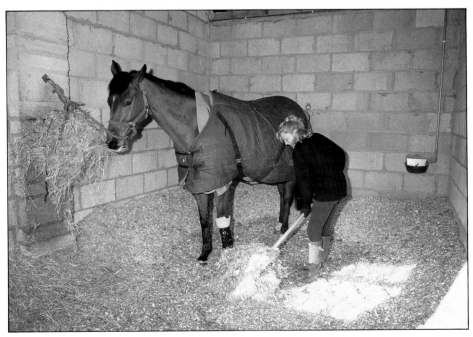

Stabling: boarding out

If you are unable to keep your horse at home, you will need to choose one of the different forms of livery provided by specialist boarding stables and riding schools.

Word-of-mouth is the best way to find a boarding stable, but if you do not know people who can advise you, have a look in the local business telephone directory, local papers and equestrian magazines. Visit a stable before deciding to send your horse there, and have a good look around the facilities provided and the other horses. See whether the horses look well and happy, the stable is well organized, tidy and safe, and the stalls are an adequate size, well ventilated and in a good state of repair. In addition, a boarding stable should have a friendly and professional atmosphere. You will probably be spending a considerable amount of time there and it is important that you enjoy it

If the stable matches up to your expectations, discuss what type of board you want, and any other requirements for your horse, with the owner.

Full board

Full board means that you pay for someone else to provide full-time care for your horse. It is an ideal arrangement for people who, due to their studies or a busy job, are very short of time. It is also a good arrangement for first-time owners who are worried about their lack of experience. The drawbacks are that it is expensive, and because you spend so little time looking after your horse, you do not get the opportunity to build up the special relationship that is part of the joy of owning a horse.

A busy stable (left)

A row of boxstalls provide these horses with plenty to look at so they do not become bored.

Palm Beach, USA (above)

The interior of a modern stable block that houses a large number of horses. Although it is very busy, good organization helps everything run smoothly.

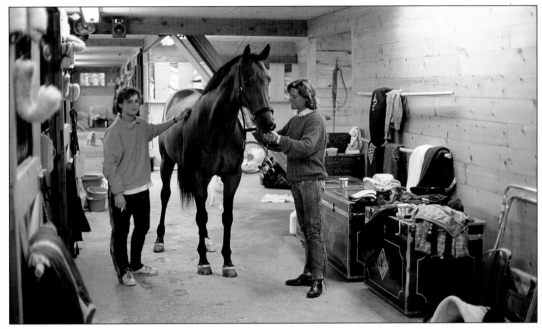

A modern stable block (left)

A well-equipped large modern stable block.

Good fencing (below)

Good post and rail fencing has been used to create a series of small paddocks.

Stabling: part-board

Part-board is less expensive than full, but more time-consuming. In return for a reduced fee, you will undertake some of the duties involved in looking after your horse yourself. Usually, you can agree with the stable owner over who does what, but you will certainly be expected to exercise your horse yourself.

Working board

This again is less expensive than full board. Working board is run by riding schools, which charge a reduced fee in return for the horse being available for lessons.

This can work well in a reputable, approved school, and you will have the bonus that your horse will be schooled for you. However, you may not want your horse to be ridden by many different people.

Self-care boarding

Under this arrangement, you pay for the use of a stable, grazing, and perhaps a tack and feed room. Everything else you do yourself, so you need to have as much time as you would if you were keeping the horse at home. The advantages of this type of boarding are, firstly, that you are able to get to know your horse as if you were keeping it at home; secondly, if you are in a shared barn, that you can usually organize a rota system with the other owners.

Pasture board

This is cheap, and is adequate if you are buying a hardy, native breed which can stand living out. There must be some form of shelter, and access to stabling in case the horse becomes ill.

Indoor stalls

This form of stabling, where each horse has its own compartment within one large building, provides plenty of daylight and fresh air.

Preparing for a ride (left)

Some riding schools take in horses at a reduced fee on the basis that they will be ridden by clients.

Good grazing (below)

When choosing a boarding stable, check the quality of the grazing as well as the stable itself.

Stable routine

The stable, yard or barn routine is the program around which hinges all the management practices you carry out when looking after a horse. It covers the management timetable and schedule of jobs whatever system of keeping the horse you use, whether it is stabled, in pasture, or on the combined system, spending some of its day stabled and some pastured out or in a surfaced or earth yard or corral.

Horses are creatures of habit and prefer to do more or less the same things at the same time each day. In practice, however, this is often not possible; for example, competition horses have a significantly different routine on show days than on other days. Sometimes entire days may be spent traveling. Even riding-school horses who work mainly on their home premises cannot be guaranteed to be ridden at the same times each day.

It is important, nevertheless, to have some kind of routine which the horse can trust, and it is quite possible to compromise by adapting your 'at home' routine on working days. For example, many show-jumping riders exercise and school their horses in the afternoon rather than the mornings, as is more usual, since jumping classes at shows are normally held in the afternoon.

Most important is to try to feed, exercise and groom at the same times each day as nearly as possible, as this will keep the horse settled, calm and therefore able to work better.

Two sample routines are given for horses kept on the combined system, one for working and one for non-working owners. Adapt these routines to suit your own hours and your horse's normal work-time patterns. Provided that feeding times are maintained and work times are kept to a routine during the week, the horse will not be disorientated by changes at the weekend or on working days. A common fault is to miss out a horse's midday feed (if it is used to having one) on a show day. This can upset a horse mentally and physically, so be sure to at least let it graze when you get the chance during a break in proceedings.

Schooling

A schooling or exercising session needs to be fitted in to the routine at the same time each day.

Sample routine for a working owner	Sample routine for a non-working owner
Early morning	**Early morning**
Check horse. Quarter, pick out feet. If exercising, tack up and exercise. On return, feed. While horse is eating, put away tack, make up rest of day's feeds/haynets, and put supply of hay in field if the grazing is poor. Put on turn-out rug, if needed, and turn horse out. Muck out/skip out stable. Leave midday feed for helper to give, if appropriate.	Check horse, feed, provide small hay ration, check water. Go for own breakfast.
	Quarter/pick out feet, tack up and exercise. On return, turn out horse, with hay supply if necessary. Muck out stable, clean tack. Perform any other routine jobs that are necessary.
Evening	
Bring horse in and check over. Quarter/groom, pick out feet and check shoes. Give feed, check water supply and leave generous hay ration.	**Late afternoon**
	Put feed and hay ready in box, check water supply. Bring in horse and groom, if dry. If wet, put on anti-sweat rug under ordinary blanket or use modern 'breathable'-fabric blanket; groom when dry.
Late evening, if possible	
Feed, water and leave enough hay to last until one or two hours before morning exercise.	**Late evening, if possible**
	Check horse. Remove droppings and replenish bedding if necessary. Feed, water and fill up haynet. Rug up appropriately for the season, if necessary.
Weekends	
Full muck out. A very thorough grooming or shampoo. Clean tack.	

Cleaning up (below)

The stable yard must be kept clean and tidy at all times.

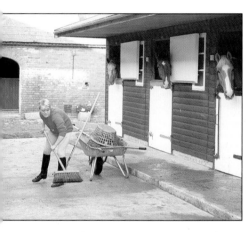

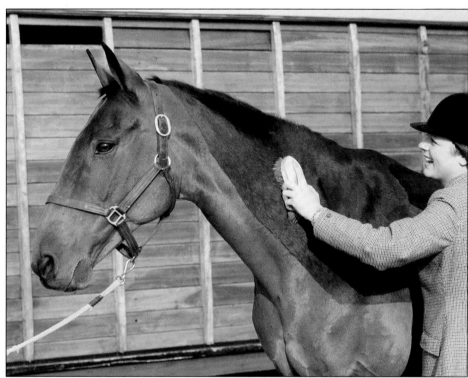

Grooming (above)

Grooming is a natural, social activity for the horse, and helps to create a bond between the horse and its owner.

Show time (left)

Even at a show, try to keep as closely as you can to the routine that the horse is used to.

Grooming

Grooming is a time when horse and owner can form the strongest of bonds. It is a very personal process, of course. You are making contact with every part of the horse's body, not only in areas where herd members would not reach during natural social grooming, but in a different and very thorough way. In nature, for example, the horse would never have its face sponged, its sheath washed out or be body-brushed to remove most of the natural grease in its coat.

Grooming is necessary and important in domesticated, and particularly stabled, animals to keep the skin clean and functioning well. Pastured and combined-system horses are out in the rain, which cleans the coat and skin to some extent. However, in other ways they get dirtier than stabled horses. They roll in mud, partly to 'dust' the coat and make it less desirable to skin parasites, partly to give themselves a stiff, wind-proof protection of dried mud, and partly as a social practice. (Horses usually pick special rolling spots. These retain the 'herd odor' and help with bonding and identification.)

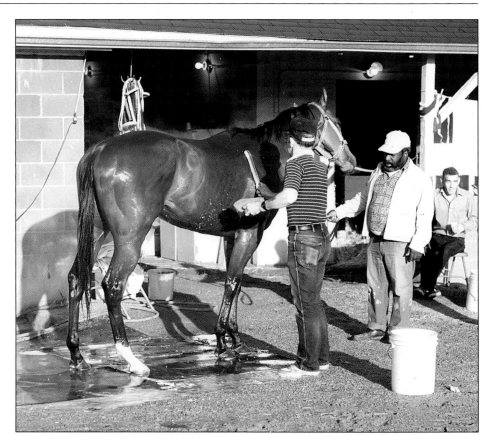

Washing down

In hot climates horses will enjoy a good hose down.

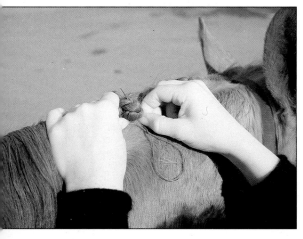

Braiding

Braiding the horse's mane is an essential part of the preparations for a show.

Natural grooming reinforces social bonding, and so does the grooming done by the owner. However, the latter may not be so keen for the horse to mutual-groom back! If your horse starts to scrape your shoulder or back with its teeth, do not mistake this for biting. Although older horses learn that this is not normally wanted, you should let your horse nuzzle you with its lips during grooming and other close contact to let it express its affection and closeness with you.

If a horse is difficult to groom, do not force the issue. It may have been roughly treated in the past and now resents the process, fearing further discomfort or even browbeating from its handler. Be gentle but slightly persistent, and reassuring with your voice, and be content with a little improvement daily.

Even with a stabled horse, it is not essential to groom thoroughly every day if you are desperately busy. Feeding, watering and exercising are more important, and keeping the ground condition free from manure.

Groom to a routine, doing the same parts in the same order each time so the horse gets used to it, knows what to expect, and so that you do not miss anything. Test your work by rubbing up the hair the wrong way, hard, wearing white gloves. Areas most often neglected are under the mane and forelock, under the jaw and belly, between the legs, the back of the pasterns and under the tail.

If the horse is specially worried about sensitive areas such as the head or belly, where the skin is thinnest, be satisfied with using just a stable rubber or even your hands, and progress gradually day by day.

Grooming (left)

Some people insist on tying up a horse for grooming, but it is a sign of good manners and trust if the horse does not need this except, of course, if it is done outdoors.

Clipping (below)

Horses with thick coats need to be clipped in winter if they are engaged in serious competitive work. It will prevent them from getting too hot and losing condition through excess sweating.

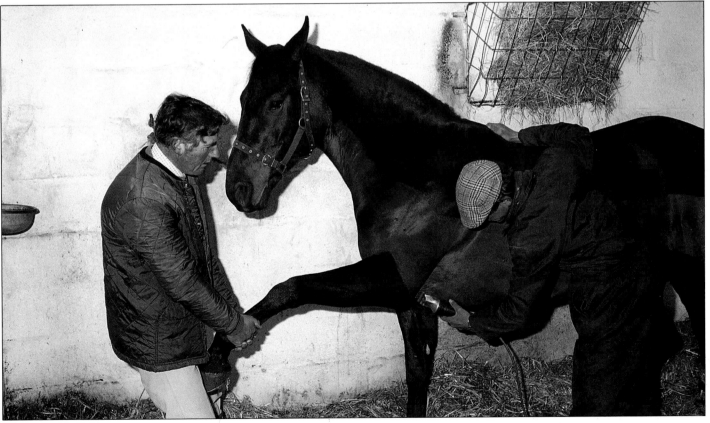

Feeding

Feeding is the single most important topic in horse management. A horse that is correctly fed for its level of work, the weather, and its constitution and temperament is best placed to work at its best, feel good and be resistant to disease. A malnourished horse – and this means not only a horse fed unsufficient quantities of food, but one fed on an imbalanced diet – does not get the best from its feed, may never reach optimum physical strength and performance, will not feel well, will not be as resistant to disease and may even be made sick by faulty nutrition.

Horses at grass are just as prone to poor dietary management as stabled horses because pasture can vary in quality and nutritional content according to geographical location, the time of year, the grasses and herbs present (or absent) and the level and quality of management given to it.

Horses evolved to eat a little food more or less round the clock. Left to themselves, they will eat for about 16 hours out of 24. This way, they not only get the nutrients they need, but feel comfortable too.

Feeding for fitness

A horse needs to be fed correctly if it is to achieve optimum fitness and performance.

Hay

A haynet is the most efficient and economical way to feed hay.

Although one of the best-known rules of feeding is 'little and often', in practice this is often not possible. The standard three feeds a day with hay (or some other roughage fodder such as hayage or fodder straw) given only night and morning does not constitute little and often, and some nutritionists believe it to be one major cause of 'unexplained' colic.

The horse's digestive system works by means not only of enzymes, which break down the feed to make it more easily absorbed into the bloodstream, but also by means of a large bacteria population which lives in the horse's gut and helps to digest the food that the horse eats. The bacteria also need a frequent supply of balanced, high-quality nutrients or they die off in large numbers leaving too few to carry out digestion. The result is indigestion and, possibly, serious illness in the horse.

No matter how hard a horse is working, it needs an ample supply of bulky roughage such as hay or a hay substitute to give the necessary feeling of fullness and satisfaction and to help physically break up the concentrate part of the ration for easier processing by digestive juices and bacteria.

The only way to be certain of the entire diet's energy level and nutritional content is to have it analysed or expertly assessed by a qualified consultant such as your veterinary surgeon or a nutritionist. This should only be needed occasionally to give you a basis to work on, and allow for variation according to the horse's work/rest pattern.

To gauge the total weight of food your horse needs per day, you first need to find out its weight. The most accurate way of doing this is obviously to get the horse weighed on a weighbridge, but another reliable method is to use a tape such as Equitape, which is available from feed merchants and some good saddlers.

Once you know its weight, feed your horse for, say, active riding club activities or active riding out, at the rate per day of 2½ per cent of its bodyweight in total feed weight. For example, if your horse turns out to weigh 453.5 kg (1000 lb) you would feed it 11.3 kg (25 lb) of food daily. For this type of work, split this into two-thirds bulky

roughage (hay) and one-third concentrates. Obviously, alter the proportions should the work increase or decrease (but never below 50/50 roughage/concentrates), and always decrease concentrates before decreasing work, and increase work before increasing concentrates.

Forget the old practice of feeding a bran mash once weekly as this constitutes a sudden change of feeding which can kill off digestive bacteria and reduce digestive efficiency. Laxatives should not be necessary with correctly fed animals. If you want to feed a no-concentrate manger feed, give instead molassed chop with some dried grass meal and thoroughly soaked sugar beet pulp, if your horse is used to such ingredients.

It is safest to give some of every ingredient (cubes, coarse mix, oats, barley, chop, roots or whatever you use) in each feed so that the bacteria receive a constant supply of food, only varying the amounts according to work. So for a mash equivalent as described in the previous paragraph, include just a single handful of its normal concentrate.

Do not feed any vitamin/mineral supplement without taking expert advice. Not only could your horse not need it, the wrong supplement could cause problems.

Your horse should have a constant supply of hay and clean water except for one, or at most two, hours before work, if it is to remain content mentally and physically, and keep its digestive system constantly occupied, as it must be for optimum health.

Grazing (above)

However good the pasture, it will not by itself provide the nutrients needed by a fit, working horse.

Giving a feed (right)

The horse's feeds are best given in a fixed manger. It should be at chest height and should lift out for cleaning.

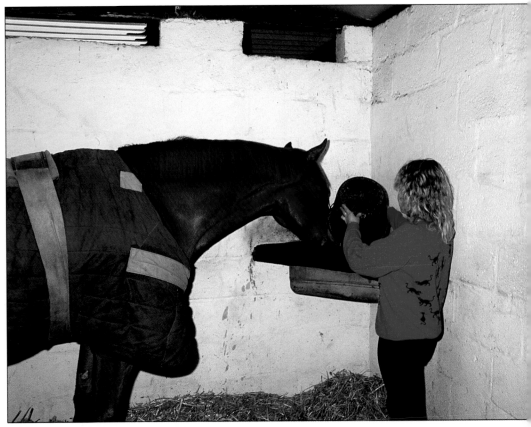

Tack and clothing

Tack and horse clothing are expensive items, and deserve good care because of that. But more importantly, poorly maintained, low-quality tack is prone to excessive wear, breaks without warning (so causing accidents), and often fits poorly despite all efforts to adjust it.

A high-quality saddle and bridle are sound buys; and good used items are better investments, and will give more satisfaction during use, than new poorer-quality ones. Many reputable saddlers stock second-hand items. It is a good plan always to buy tack and clothing from a member of an equestrian trade association, whose logos should be displayed on the premises or the catalogues and stationery of the firm concerned. Then you should be assured not only of expert advice but a good after-sales

service for repairs and readjustments such as saddle restuffing.

Most owners will want blankets of some kind. Two good-quality, well-fitting New Zealand or turn-out blankets are a boon to working owners who may need to leave their horses out for long winter days while they are at work. Two good stable blankets, and maybe underblankets, will be needed in winter for stabled, clipped, working animals and those required to travel. Two of each item ensures that one is always available for use while the other is laundered.

Protective boots and bandages will be required for animals needing leg protection during active work, those prone to hitting themselves, and those requiring extra warmth. It is said that a set of stable bandages is equal to an extra blanket.

Keeping the horse warm and comfortable is an essential part of keeping it mentally content and therefore in an amenable and co-operative frame of mind. It also ensures best use of its feed (by ensuring that it is not going too much towards keeping the horse warm, but is available for energy and health maintenance). You should always remember that the horse is unable to remove an uncomfortable blanket or a tail bandage that cuts into it. Strict attention to comfort, which is achieved only through a really correct fit, is therefore essential if the horse is not to be made anxious and irritable by constant discomfort from a blanket which cuts into its withers, rubs its shoulders or constantly slips round annoying it and leaving it cold.

The type and fit of tack used has a

Day blanket (above)

Woollen day blankets are worn for warmth in the stable, and when the horse is traveling.

New Zealand rugs (right)

New Zealand rugs are made of waterproof canvas part-lined with wool. They have straps to keep them in place.

Tack room (above)

A well-organized tack room is essential for the smooth running of a stable.

Boxing a horse (left)

When traveling, a horse should be wearing a day blanket or sheet, and protective leg and tail bandages.

tremendous bearing on the horse's willingness and ability to perform and, in the case of bridles, bits and schooling accessories, on its very understanding of what you want. Communication is vital during work. The use of a martingale or schooling rein, for instance, can greatly change the effect and feel of the bit and, therefore, the horse's reaction to it. Generally, the simplest arrangement commensurate with understanding and control should be used, and each partnership assessed by an expert teacher before anything stronger or more unusual is applied.

All equipment must be comfortable if the horse is not to be irritated. Irritation leads to temper, lack of co-operation, understandable rebelliousness and subsequent dangerous lack of control. Ensure that all items fit properly, that they are put on correctly, neither too tightly nor too loosely, and are kept not only in good repair, for safety's sake, but also soft and smooth for comfort. Also ensure that there is no creased-up fabric, bits of bedding or dried mud between equipment and horse, which will annoy it and make it sore.

Health

All aspects of horse management are aimed at keeping them in good health. Without basic good health, you cannot get a horse physically fit for work, it will not be mentally attuned to co-operating or absorbing schooling, and will not have the willingness or spirit to try its best. Under pressure it may become sulky, start playing up or refusing, or simply be unable to perform.

A simple daily check of your horse's health takes only a few minutes and should be part of your routine. A reasonably experienced person can tell at a glance whether or not a horse is its normal self. Its coat should be bright and smooth, even in a pasture-kept animal, its eyes bright and questing with an interested expression on its face, and ears flicking towards anything that catches its attention. It should move freely, there should be no discharges from eyes or nostrils, no swellings or 'hot spots' anywhere, and the horse should show no undue sensitivity to being handled (which could indicate soreness or pain).

Its appetite should be normal for it, and its droppings consistent and formed according to how it is kept: a pasture-kept horse will have greener, slightly looser droppings than a fully stabled horse, whose droppings will probably be khaki-coloured and formed into apple-sized balls which just break on hitting the ground. Droppings which are very dark, pale, mucus-coated, blood-streaked or offensive in smell indicate disorder, as do very hard or very sloppy droppings.

Coughing sends chills down most owners' spines. It can be a simple clearing of the throat or a sign of respiratory disease or allergy, both of which can permanently impair, or even ruin, a horse's ability to perform. A sharp, hard cough may signify a throat irritation while a softer one could be influenza and a deep, harsh one a sign of an allergy (usually in the lungs). Unless you are certain that the cough is just a throat-clearing exercise, it is always safest to call the vet. You should do so anyway if the horse coughs habitually.

Behavior is a good indicator of how a horse is feeling. If it hangs away from other horses, lies down for more than about 30 minutes at a time, seems dopey or, conversely, agitated and showing classic signs of, say, colic, call the vet.

In the case of lameness, 24 hours' box rest might clear up a slight injury, but if it does not, or if the lameness is marked, again call the vet.

Temperature, pulse and respiration rates are excellent, simple means of testing your horse's general health. The normal temperature of a horse is very near 38°C (100.4°F), pulse about 34 to 42 per minute and respiration about 8 to 14 breaths (in and out) per minute. They all increase with exercise, but in a healthy, fairly fit horse, should be back near normal within an hour. They will be naturally higher in young animals and ponies and lower in older animals. Your vet or a good instructor can show you how to take them, and instructions are given in many good management and veterinary books.

Being able to give these rates, plus any other observations about your horse's condition and behavior can greatly help your vet to assess what is wrong when disease strikes, and also helps him or her give you emergency instructions over the telephone when necessary.

Saddle sores

Saddle sores should be treated by dabbing them with surgical spirit on a pad of cotton wool.

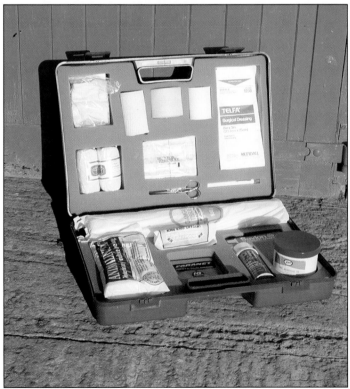

Cuts and grazes (left)

Antiseptic powder is applied to a leg wound.

The veterinary surgeon (below)

The vet checks that the horse's hind legs are sound. As soon as you buy a horse, make contact with a local vet as you will certainly need his advice and help from time to time.

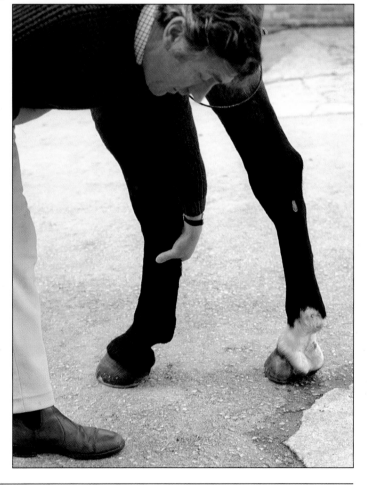

First aid box (above)

You should keep a first aid box in the tack room. Your vet will advise you on what to keep in it. Make sure that you check it regularly in case anything needs replacing.

SECTION

2

HORSE AND RIDER

RIDING TECHNIQUES
·
LEISURE RIDING

Settling down (right)

If your horse tends to get over-excited when you start a schooling session, lunge it first as this will settle it down.

Practicing at home (left)

You must be able to be self-critical when you are working on your own. If a problem occurs, do not automatically blame the horse. It may be an error on your part that is causing the problem.

By improving your basic riding skills, you can improve your communication with the horse, and increase your, and your horse's, enjoyment of the sport.

A weak link in the understanding and communication between horse and rider can have adverse effects. However, if you take the time to learn how and why your horse reacts as it does, your effectiveness as a rider will be greatly improved.

As a rider, you communicate with the horse with the aids – seat, hands, legs and voice – backed up with whip and spurs if necessary. However, it is equally important that you understand how the horse communicates with

you. If the horse puts its ears back, fights the bit, tosses its head, swishes its tail, or shows other signs of bad temper or disobedience, you must take into account that it may be confused or unbalanced by your instructions, or in discomfort for some reason.

Horses are very sensitive to their handler's moods and emotions. Any tenseness or indecision on your part will immediately be picked up by your horse. For this reason, you should never make an issue out of something that goes wrong, because the horse can be badly upset by such behavior.

Schooling at home (above)

When schooling at home, try to work in a clearly marked out area, even if you only mark the four corners.

Variety (right)

Horses can become bored and jaded by doing too much of the same thing. If a schooling session is not going well, give it a rest for the day and take the horse out for a ride instead.

RIDING TECHNIQUES

To be successful, the training of any animal must take into account the animal's natural instincts, way of thinking and view of the world. Horses learn through repetition and reward. They understand routine, and have excellent memories, and these factors should help you to understand your horse's behavior.

Some horses have very strong and dominant personalities, and they should be treated with tact and firmness. Horses that are timid, or less intelligent, should be treated with sympathy and patience. Observe your horse carefully so that you understand how it thinks and what type of personality it has.

You should be logical in your thinking and training plan – if a horse's schooling follows a logical sequence, it is possible to go back a step if a problem occurs. This will ensure that the basics are well established before you attempt more difficult lessons. By following this approach, you should be able to solve any problems before they become too serious.

Understanding the horse

It is important to understand the horse's natural instincts.

Developing a relationship (left)

You should spend time getting to know your horse in order that the two of you develop an understanding of each other.

Training (below)

Horses learn by repetition. Training should follow a logical plan. This way problems can be ironed out as you go along.

Observing your horse (left)

Study your horse closely so that you know and understand its personality.

The rider's position

A riding position has evolved that gives the rider security and the best possible chance of communicating with the horse. At the same time, it allows the horse to balance itself properly under the rider.

The horse's center of gravity is just behind its withers, which is why you sit there. Your weight should remain over the horse's center of gravity at all times if the horse is to keep its balance.

A good seat gives you the basis for an effective riding position. You should sit in the central, deepest part of the saddle, in the middle of a triangle made up of the two seatbones at the back and the fork at the front. When sitting correctly, your weight will be in the middle of the triangle.

You should aim for an independent seat, that is, being able to keep your balance in the saddle without having to cling on with your hands or legs. Your knees and thighs should remain relaxed; if you use them to grip, it will make your whole position stiff.

If you sit straight and balanced in the saddle, with arms and hands relaxed, and legs wrapped around the horse's sides, you will be able to communicate effectively with the horse using your hands, legs and seat. If you sit crookedly or unevenly in the saddle, or lean forwards or backwards, you will not be able to use your legs properly to give instructions to the horse.

The classic riding position

The rider is sitting with her weight in the center of the saddle. This puts her pelvis in the correct position, and allows her hip joint to be open. This in turn puts her legs in the correct position. Her legs lie as close as possible round the horse's sides, but without any tension. The thigh must lie as flat as possible against the saddle. The ball of the foot rests on the stirrup iron, giving the rider something to balance on and allowing her to push her weight down through her heel. Her heel is slightly lower than her toe. Her spine is straight and relaxed, so that the horse's movement can be absorbed by the hips and back. Her arms are relaxed at the shoulder and elbow so that they can move with the movement of the horse's head. The rider's hands join the arm to the reins – think of the arm and rein as belonging to the horse so they can follow its movement. The hands should be held with palms facing each other and thumbs uppermost. The rider carries her head straight but without tension.

Common faults

Stiffness

The rider's position is correct but her arms are stiff, making her tense in the saddle. This tension is transmitted to the horse, who raises its head in apprehension.

Leaning back

The rider's pelvis is tipped back so there is too much weight on her seatbones. As a result her legs have come forward and her back has rounded. She will find it difficult to use her lower leg effectively, and she will be unable to absorb the horse's movement and stay in balance with it.

Tipping forward

The rider's pelvis is tipped forward, and she is sitting too much on her fork. As a result her body is leaning forwards, and her legs have moved too far back, putting her out of alignment with the horse's center of gravity.

Achieving the correct position

The rider's weight is balanced over the horse's centre of gravity, and the shoulder, hip and heel are in a straight line.

Annkathrin Linsenhoff

A good position in the saddle is the basis of all communication with the horse, enabling the rider to ask the horse to perform complicated manoeuvres at different paces.

The rider's position

Advanced movements

In order to execute advanced dressage movements, you have to be able to make subtle and imperceptable adjustments to your position, slightly shifting your weight in the saddle, thus indicating to the horse what is wanted. This is only possible if you first develop a good, independent seat with your weight evenly distributed.

Back view

The rider's elbows are tucked in and bent but without showing any tension. Her lower legs are in contact with the horse's sides and the stirrup leathers are perpendicular to the ground.

Front view

The rider's legs are close around the horse with her knees and thighs relaxed. The rider maintains a conversation with the horse by keeping her lower legs and ankles in contact with its sides.

The basis of communication

A good position in the saddle is the basis for all communication with the horse.

Common faults

Sitting crooked: 1

The rider is sitting with her weight over to the right and has collapsed her left hip. This will make it difficult for her to communicate clearly with the horse, and will unbalance the horse. It may also make the horse uneven and give it back problems.

Sitting crooked: 2

The rider is right off balance. She is putting too much weight on her right seatbone and her left leg has compensated by sticking out from the horse's side. The horse will have a fright when the rider's left leg is applied to it. In addition, she will have to stiffen in order to stay in the saddle.

The aids

The rider gives the horse instructions by means of the aids. There are two types: the natural aids – the rider's seat, hands, legs and voice; and the artificial aids – spurs, whips and some items of tack such as martingales (see Artificial aids, page 88).

The hands and legs operate in combination with each other and should be applied in a co-ordinated way. There is little point in using your legs to tell the horse to walk on if your hands are stiff and resistant to its moving.

You must be able to use each hand and leg independently. Your inside hand controls the horse's direction, your outside hand controls the pace, your inside leg creates impulsion, and your outside leg controls the horse's hindquarters so that they don't swing out.

To create impulsion you make use of the fact that a horse always moves away from the rider's leg. If you apply pressure to the horse's sides by closing your lower legs against it, the horse will move forwards away from the pressure. If you apply pressure on one side only the horse will move away from that leg.

In order to control and make use of the energy created by your legs, you use your hands to contain the horse's forward movement, thereby creating an active pace in the horse. You need to have an independent seat (see page 66) in order to use your legs properly and be free of your hands, that is, not leaning on them for balance.

You must be aware of how you feel to the horse. If your contact is too strong or too light, it will let you know by carrying its head incorrectly, by chewing its bit, in the way it moves, and even by going faster to try to get away from the discomfort.

Your voice can calm and reassure the horse, or reprimand it. The horse will come to recognize the tone of voice and even some commands.

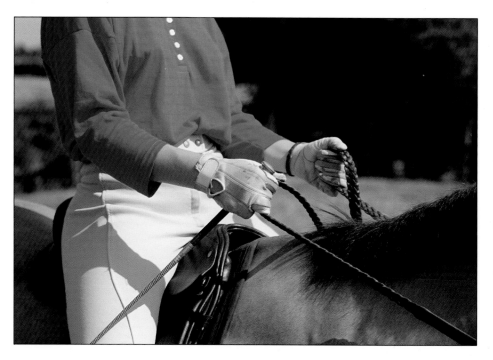

Sympathetic hands

The horse's mouth is very sensitive, and your hands must be sympathetic if it is not to become hardened or damaged. You hold the reins by wrapping the fingers around the rein, almost closing the hands to make a fist. This gives you a firm grip on the reins without having to use your arms. The arms remain soft and relaxed. The horse's movement is contained by putting pressure on the bit through the reins. The severity of the aid will depend, to some extent, on the sensitivity of the horse. You must match what the horse offers you.

Applying the leg aids: basic position

Your lower leg should be in contact with the horse's side all the time. To apply the leg, you close your lower leg and ankle against the horse's side, still using the inside of the leg, not the back of the heel.

Creating impulsion

The inside lower leg is applied on the girth to create impulsion and to instruct the horse to bend around that leg when making turns and circles.

Common faults

Uneven hands

If the rider's hands are uneven, the bit will not lie correctly in the horse's mouth, and the tension on its mouth will be wrongly distributed.

Restrictive hands

The horse is reacting to a stiff arm and unyielding hand by tilting its head, grinding its bit, putting its ears back and refusing to walk on actively. The rider's stiffness is causing the problem, which can be solved by work on developing a secure, independent seat.

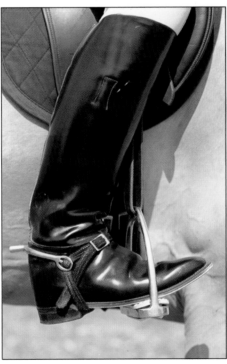

Common faults

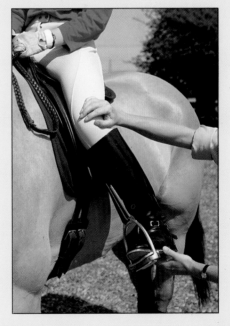

Controlling the hindquarters

The outside lower leg is applied behind the girth, to make sure that the hindquarters do not swing out but follow the line of the front end.

The position of the foot

The stirrup iron is under the ball of the foot, and the heel is lower than the toe. This makes it easier to apply the legs correctly. You may have difficulty at first in keeping the heel below the toe.

Leg sticking out

Do not ride with your lower leg sticking out from the horse. If you try to apply the leg aids from this position, your horse will have a bad fright.

The walk

The walk is a four-beat gait with four even beats to every stride. The horse picks up and puts down each leg separately.

In walk, aim for a free, easy rhythm, with even, unhurried strides. Use the inside leg to create impulsion while the outside leg holds the hindquarters in place. The horse nods its head in order to balance itself, and you must allow this movement with your hands to let the horse take a full stride. Sit as still as you can in the saddle and stay relaxed so that your body absorbs the horse's movement, and use your legs in rhythm with its pace. Try to develop an awareness of how the horse moves in the walk, and how your own position affects its movement.

You can maintain a good position more easily in the walk than in any of the other gaits. However, it is also the easiest of the gaits to destroy by bad riding. If you restrict the horse's movement with your hands you will put it off balance and cause it to shorten its stride. If you push it on too hard it will lose its rhythm, and may start to jog because its balance is upset.

A good walk

The rider (top) is using her inside leg to create good forward movement and at the same time is maintaining a steady contact with the horse's mouth. It knows it is not going to be jabbed in the mouth by the bit, so it is going forwards confidently into the rider's controlling hands.

Free walk

The rider (above) drops the reins so that the horse can stretch out as it walks. This is a good way to reward a horse and allow it to relax when it has been working strongly in walk and trot.

Common faults

Loss of contact

The rider has let her reins go, losing all contact with the horse's mouth. She is slouching in the saddle and is not pushing the horse on with her leg. As a result the horse is ambling along with its head dropped, rather than walking out with even steps.

Stiffness

The rider's arms are straight and stiff, her hands are too low, and they are not giving with the horse's movement. The horse is fighting against this restriction by raising its head and tipping it to one side.

Jogging

The rider has crept up the horse's neck so that her weight is a long way out of place, and she is holding the horse on a very short rein. This makes the horse anxious and it starts to jog.

1

2

3

4

4

2

3

1

The walk – a four-beat gait

The sequence of footfalls is: (1) near hind, (2) near fore, (3) off hind, (4) near fore.

The trot

The trot is a two-beat gait. The horse moves its legs in diagonal pairs: the off fore and near hind, the right diagonal, move together; and the near fore and off hind, the left diagonal, move together. In between, there is a moment of suspension as the horse springs from one diagonal to another.

The rider can either sit to the trot, trying to absorb the movement of the horse through the hips and back; or rise to the trot, sitting and rising on alternate diagonals. When doing a rising trot you should have your feet lightly balanced in the stirrups, your lower leg wrapped around the horse, and you should rise with the horse's movement. Use your inside leg to create impulsion as you sit, and contain the movement by keeping a good contact with the hands.

A common problem in trot is lack of activity on the horse's part. You have to learn, through trial and error, the correct balance between the amount of pressure to apply with the leg, and the amount to contain with the hands to produce the desired result with each individual horse. On the other hand, if you create too much impulsion and force the pace, the horse will become worried and stiffen up.

You should aim for a general impression of suppleness and elasticity, with the horse taking active, regular steps. The hind legs should be actively engaged, taking the horse's weight and creating the forward movement.

A good trot

The rider uses her legs to create impulsion and the horse steps out well. Its hind leg comes well underneath its body, showing that its hindquarters are engaged and working actively.

The trot – a two-beat gait

In trot the sequence of footfalls is: (1) and (2) off fore and near hind together; (3) and (4) near fore and off hind together.

Common faults

Leaning back

The rider is behind the horse's movement. Her body is no longer upright, her arms have become stiff and she is balancing by hanging on to the reins. In response the horse has raised its head and neck and indicates that it is not comfortable with the rider's position.

Loose reins

The rider has let her reins go long and is sitting too far forward. The energy she is creating by using her legs is wasted as she has lost contact with the horse's mouth and therefore cannot contain the horse's movement. As a result, the horse's weight is falling onto its forehand.

Uphill trot

Hillwork should be included in your training program because it gets a horse fit.

The canter

The canter is the most natural gait for a horse. It is a three-beat movement, with the three beats and then a moment of suspension.

The horse should be cantering with even strides, with rhythm and impulsion, in a nicely balanced outline, its head, neck, back, hindquarters and hocks making a good, rounded shape. It should be light on its forehand, its hindquarters supporting its weight and creating the movement.

The rider sits down in the saddle for all three beats, pushing with the seat and squeezing with the lower legs on the first beat of each stride to create impulsion. In canter, as in walk, the horse nods its head up and down, and the rider's hands must allow this movement.

Riders sometimes find it difficult to sit to the canter and absorb the movement through their hips. This will be easier if you can learn how the correct seat feels so that you know what you are trying to achieve. When you are in the enclosed space of a schooling ring, ask your horse to canter. Put both reins into the outside hand and hold on to the back of the saddle with your inside hand. This brings your body back over your seat bones so you can experience what it feels like to sit in the saddle for all three beats.

A good canter

The horse's hind legs are active, its strides are even and it is working in a good outline. The rider is absorbing the movement with her hips and back, and keeping a steady contact with the horse's mouth.

Getting fit (right)

Work at the canter is a good way to get a horse fit and improves its balance.

Common faults

Weight on the forehand

The horse's hindlegs are not coming underneath it and its weight has fallen onto its forehand. This has happened because the rider is behind the movement, so she cannot use her legs properly to push the horse on.

Restrictive hands

This can be caused by tension or lack of confidence in the rider. Her arms and elbows are stiff and her hands are set rigid, restricting the horse's movement. It has shortened its outline, and its strides lack impulsion and rhythm.

Stiffness

The rider is perching stiffly on top of the saddle. The horse is reacting against this by raising its head and hollowing its outline, and it cannot bring its hindquarters under it sufficiently. As a result the canter loses impulsion and balance.

1

2

3

4

2

3

1

4

The canter – a three-beat gait

In canter to the left the sequence of footfalls is: (1) off hind; (2) off fore and near hind together; (3) near fore. After this point all four feet leave the ground (4).

Upward transitions

Changes of gait are called transitions. Upward transitions involve going up a gait: walk to trot and trot to canter. Downward transitions involve coming down a gait (see Downward transitions, page 80). The success of a transition relies on the quality of the gait that comes before it. You must prepare the horse and yourself for a transition in order to make a good one.

The horse must be balanced, and responding well to your commands, and you must create sufficient impulsion to carry you into the next gait. If you do not have enough impulsion, the horse will lift itself into the next gait. A feeling for the correct amount of impulsion comes with experience, and varies from horse to horse.

To make a transition, maintain a good position in the saddle and keep a good contact through the hands with the horse's mouth. Ask for the change of gait by sitting down in the saddle and closing your legs around the horse's sides. Maintain a firm but sympathetic contact with the horse's mouth throughout the change of gait. if you do not, the horse will just go faster rather than moving up a pace.

Do not be tempted to lean forward in an upward transition, as you will go into the gait ahead of the horse. You must remain in balance with the horse in order to go with it as it takes the first step in the new gait.

Walk to trot

The rider's position is good. She is maintaining a firm contact with the horse's mouth and is keeping a conversation going with the horse via her legs. The horse is balanced and is stepping out well.

Trot to canter

For the transition from trot to canter you should be in sitting trot, with the horse balanced underneath you. Resist the temptation to lean forward; sit down in the saddle and close your legs against the horse. It is best to move into canter as you approach a corner coming down the long side of the school.

Common faults: walk to trot

Lack of communication through the legs (left)

The rider's legs are away from the horse's sides, completely out of contact with the horse, so the instruction to change gait surprises it. The rider has let the reins go loose as well. The horse reacts by hollowing its outline and shortening its steps.

Getting ahead of the horse (right)

The rider has anticipated the transition by tipping forwards and dropping contact with the reins. As a result there is no controlling hand for the horse to go forwards into. It jumps into the next gait rather than stepping forwards into it.

Unresponsive to the leg (left)

The rider has failed to achieve a good, active pace before the transition, and is also leaning forwards. As a result, the transition is sluggish.

Lack of preparation (right)

The rider has let the reins go loose, losing contact with the horse's mouth, and she is not creating impulsion in the horse's hindquarters. The horse's weight is on its forehand, and the transition is poor.

Common faults: trot to canter

Restricting the horse

The rider is holding the horse on too tight a rein, and her hands are not allowing the movement of the horse's head. The horse is fighting against this restriction by raising its head and neck and resisting the movement.

Standing up

The rider is standing up in the saddle and leaning forwards. From this position she cannot push the horse forward into a canter.

Downward transitions

A horse's conformation is not particularly well suited to downward transitions. A horse takes the strain of halting on its hind legs. However, with a rider on top, its weight is pushed forward and its forelegs take more of the strain. In a downward transition it is easy to let the horse's weight fall on its forehand, especially if you have too much impulsion.

The half-halt can be used to prepare the horse for a downward transition. It acts as a signal from the rider that an instruction is about to be given, and it also helps in balancing the horse. You sit up in the saddle to move the weight back onto the hindquarters. Close the legs round the horse and give a little check on the outside rein while maintaining the direction of the bend with the inside rein.

To ask for a downward transition, increase the aids. Sit well down in the saddle and close your legs around the horse to bring its hocks underneath it. Keep contact on the inside rein

to maintain the bend and give the stop aid with the outside rein to check the forward movement of the horse. By driving the horse forwards into the bit you make it bring its hocks underneath it during the transition, so that its weight does not fall onto its forehand.

To bring the horse to a halt, sit well into the saddle and close your legs around it, then restrict with the hands. The hand aids are: steady on the inside rein to maintain the bend, take and let go on the outside rein to bring the horse up. Aim to get the horse's weight back on its hindquarters and move it forwards into a restraining but allowing hand. It must be a fluid movement. If the hand is too restraining, the halt will be too abrupt.

In the early stages of a horse's training all transitions should be progressive, coming down from canter to trot, trot to walk, and walk to halt. Later on, you can incorporate acute downward transitions into its training.

Preparing for a transition (above)

To assist the horse the rider maintains a good position in the saddle. She is pushing the horse on with her legs to bring its hocks underneath it, at the same time exerting strong pressure on the horse's mouth.

Completing the transition (above right)

By remaining in balance horse and rider achieve a good transition down with the horse ready to step well into the next gait.

Coming to a halt

With a young horse, aim to bring the horse up with front legs square, and hind legs nearly square.

Common faults

Tipping forward

The rider has shifted forwards. The horse has its weight on its forehand and its hindquarters are unevenly balanced. The rider was in the wrong position to communicate with the horse.

Leaning back

The rider is leaning back and pulling on the reins to bring the horse down a gait. The horse becomes resistant to the rider's action, so the gait following the transition will be affected.

Turns and circles

Although the term "bend" is used to describe the horse as it moves through a turn or circle, it does not actually bend because it has a rigid backbone. However, by doing turns and circles the horse is trained to contract its ribcage on the inside of the bend and expand its ribcage on the outside of the bend.

The aids to use to achieve this movement are: inside rein for direction, outside rein for controlling the pace and bend, inside leg for impulsion and bend, and outside leg to control the hindquarters.

Exercises on turns and circles are best done within a rectangular area marked out on the ground. It should be twice as long as it is wide, with quarter-markers on the long sides, and half-way markers on the short sides. Aim for an area about 66ft (20m) wide to start with, in order to work on 66ft (20m) diameter circles. Once your horse has become supple and balanced, you can work on smaller circles. Remember to do all exercises in both directions, so that the horse's muscles develop evenly.

"Tracking up", meaning that the horse is overstepping the hoof prints of the fore feet as it goes around the circle, is considered good because, to achieve this, the horse's hocks have to be underneath it. But it is important to remember that a long-backed horse will have considerably more difficulty in over-stepping its hoof prints than a short-coupled horse that may overstep easily without actively working its hindquarters.

Turning correctly

The rider closes the inside leg against the horse to ask it to move forwards away from the leg while using the outside leg behind the girth to prevent the horse's hindquarters swinging out. At the same time she uses the inside hand to ask the horse to turn and controls the degree of bend with the outside hand. She looks in the direction in which she wants the horse to travel. She is applying the aids in a well coordinated way to produce a good turn: the horse's head is just inclined in the direction of the movement and the hind legs are following in the path of the front legs.

Controlling the bend (above)

The object is to keep the horse looking in the direction in which it is moving. Its neck should have no more bend in it than the body.

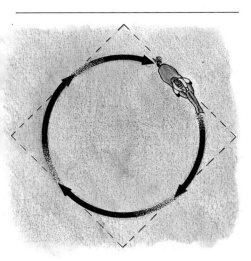

Riding circles and turns

When riding a circle, imagine a diamond shape on the ground. Ride around the diamond, rounding off each point. This should give you a correct circle. Turns consist of a section of a circle, and are ridden in the same way.

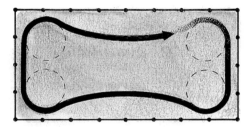

Riding loops

Shallow loops made on the long side of the area will teach the horse to change the direction of the bend and make it more supple. You can introduce a small circle at the end of the loop.

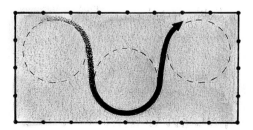

Serpentines

Once you are going well on circles and loops, you can also introduce serpentines across the width of the area into the routine.

Common faults

Looking in the wrong direction

The rider is trying to make the horse bend into the corner by holding it out with her outside hand, instead of using her legs to control the movement. As a result, the horse is looking in the wrong direction and has hollowed against the rider.

Bending too far

The horse is bending its neck too much to the inside of the circle. If the correct degree of bending is being maintained, the rider should be able to see the corner of the horse's inside eye, but this horse has far more of its head turned in.

Faulty riding position

The rider is looking too far around the circle, so her head and upper body are turned too much to the inside of the circle. The rider should be looking through her horse's ears with her shoulders and hips parallel to those of the horse.

Improver lesson: sluggish horses

If you have a sluggish horse, rather than a forward-going type, there are ways to improve its performance and make it a more enjoyable ride.

To make a sluggish horse more supple, its training is much the same as for other horses. Extra exercises, such as lengthening the stride in trot, are helpful.

In order to really improve a sluggish horse, you must teach it to be very obedient to instructions from your leg. If, when you give the horse an instruction for the first time, it does not respond ask again more firmly. If that fails, give it a tap with a whip behind your leg at the same time as you ask with your leg for the third time.

You also need to correct any positional faults which may have developed in your own riding as a result of riding a sluggish horse.

Once you have the horse going well, you can incorporate transitions into the program to sharpen up its responsiveness. Start with easier ones such as walk to halt; then move on to trot, halt, and back to trot again. Once these are being executed properly and easily the more difficult transitions of walk to canter/canter to walk, can be used.

Being behind the movement

The rider (top) has her weight back and is leaning backwards, putting her behind the movement of the horse. This makes it impossible for her to give proper instructions to the horse with her legs.

A sloppy position

The rider (above) is perching on top of the horse rather than sitting deep in the saddle. Her body is stiff, her hands are too low, her arms are straight and she has no contact through the reins with the horse's mouth. As a result the horse is ambling along.

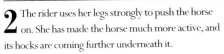

1 The rider takes up contact with the reins, and the horse is already moving on better. Her hands are giving with the movement of the horse's head.

2 The rider uses her legs strongly to push the horse on. She has made the horse much more active, and its hocks are coming further underneath it.

3 The horse becomes more responsive to the rider's instructions, and they move on to more demanding exercises.

Improver lesson: fizzy horses

A fizzy horse may be very forward going, but it must still be ridden from the leg. At the same time, the rider must have very sympathetic hands.

You need to establish whether the horse's behavior is due to its temperament or to fear. For example, if the horse's bit causes it pain, it will try to run away from it. In this case, the problem should be solved by changing to a milder one. If you are contemplating a change of bit, take advice from an experienced person.

As a fizzy horse often over-reacts to the rider's leg against its sides, riders tend to keep their legs away from it. However, it is essential that the horse is taught to accept the rider's legs on its sides so that the rider can keep a gentle conversation going.

Whatever the cause of a horse's fizzy behavior (apart from its tack), the same remedies apply. The horse's mind must be kept active by plenty of schooling. Repetitive exercises such as large circles, shallow loops, serpentines and figures-of-eight should be used to calm it. It will learn to settle down when doing these exercises, so you can use them if it becomes over-excited at a show as well.

Sitting too far forward

The rider (top) is sitting forward in the saddle, leaning forwards and propping herself up on her hands. Her leg has come away from the horse's side. As a result, the horse leans in, making it unbalanced. This gives the rider even less chance of controlling it.

Long reins

In trying not to upset the horse the rider (above) has let the reins become too long. She must take up the reins very gently so that the horse does not react violently against the restriction.

Rearing up (below)

A horse behaves badly for many different reasons. You should consider its diet, health, whether its tack is comfortable or not, and your own riding, when trying to assess the cause of problems.

Accepting the leg

1 Once you have settled the horse, you must teach it to accept instructions from your leg. Begin with spirals in and out of circles, and moving the horse away from the inside leg by putting pressure on that side. Then move on to turns on the forehand and lateral work (see pages 158-65).

2 The horse is now accepting contact from the rider's hand and leg well, and is going forward in a much better shape. It has settled down and is working in partnership with its rider.

Artificial aids

The natural aids can be reinforced by use of artificial aids if a horse is slow to respond. It is very important that the artificial aids – spurs, whips and items of tack such as martingales – are used correctly if they are to be effective in improving the rider's communication with the horse.

Spurs should always be used with caution and only by experienced riders. They should be short and blunt. Various lengths of spur are available but to stay within the rules of the various competitive bodies the neck should not exceed 3 cm (1¼ in) in length. Serrated spurs should not be worn. When fitting a spur, take care that the neck of the spur is pointing downwards.

To use the whip, tap it against the horse behind the girth to reinforce the leg aid. Until you are experienced in using a whip, however, use a short one, because it is easy to hit a horse accidentally with a long one. For jumping, a whip should be between 45 and 75 cm (17¾-29½ in).

Check your whips regularly for wear and tear as the end of a whip can easily come off. Always repair a damaged whip immediately so that it does not cut the horse.

Some horses are able to evade their rider's instructions by throwing their heads in the air so that the rider cannot control the horse effectively. Martingales are designed to prevent the horse raising its head above the point of control, in which case they exert a downward pressure on the reins (running martingale) or on the noseband (standing martingale).

Using a whip

Only use a whip when the horse does not respond to the leg aid. First ask with the leg. If the horse does not respond, tell it with the leg. If it still does not respond, tell it with the whip, applying it vertically just behind the leg.

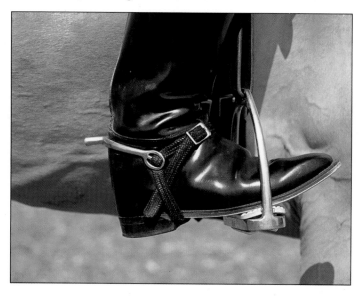

A correctly fitted spur

The spur must lie on the seam of the boot so that if the leg is in the correct position the spur will not be in contact with the horse. If the horse is slow to respond to the leg, the spur can be brought into use by the rider turning her toe out.

Wrongly fitted spur

If the spur is fitted too low on the rider's heel, it will be ineffective.

A jumping whip (left)

The short jumping whip is carried in the same way as the longer schooling whip (below).

A schooling whip (below)

The knob is pushed right down to the hand and the whip is carried lightly, lying across the rider's thigh.

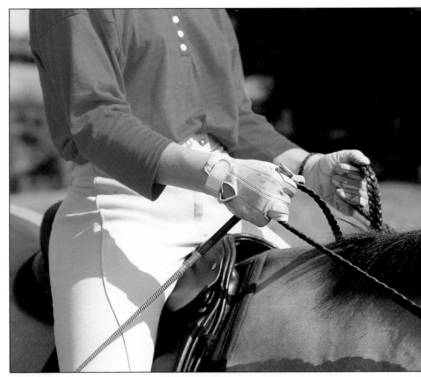

The running martingale (right)

This is the most commonly used martingale. It consists of a leather strap running from the girth to the rein, supported by a neck strap that is attached to it at the horse's chest. At the girth end, it has a loop through which the girth passes. At the other end the strap divides into two, each with a ring at the end. The reins pass through these rings. A correctly fitted running martingale will not come into effect unless the horse raises its head too high.

The standing martingale (above)

This consists of one strap, one end of which is attached to girth and neckstrap in the same way as the running martingale. The other end is attached to the noseband by a loop. It should only ever be used with a flash noseband, not any other type. The strap must be long enough from chest to noseband to reach the horse's throat if held against it.

The jumping position

When a horse jumps, it lengthens and elevates its stride. There is little elevation over small fences, but as the height increases so the horse has to make more effort to get over it and the degree of elevation increases.

On the flat the horse's center of gravity lies just behind its withers (see page 67). As the horse jumps, its centre of gravity moves forward, because the horse is stretching its head and neck forward over the fence. Your position must therefore move forward to keep your weight over the horse's center of gravity. You do this by folding forward at the hip and trying to flatten your body down close to the horse, not by leaning forwards. The size of the fence will dictate how much you need to fold. The higher the fence, the more you fold. At the same time, your legs should remain in the same position, on the girth, from take-off to landing, so that you can communicate with the horse throughout the jump.

In order to achieve this forward seat you must shorten your stirrup leathers, usually by a couple of holes, in order to reduce the angles at the hip, knee and ankle. However, as your flatwork progresses and you achieve a deeper seat on the flat, you will need to shorten your leathers more.

The correct jumping position (above)

The shortened leathers have the effect of moving your seat towards the back of the saddle so that the lower leg and knee can sit firmly around the horse . Your seat comes slightly out of the saddle and your body folds forward from the hips. Keep your back straight and look ahead. Your elbows remain bent and your hands must follow the movement of the horse's head.

The center of gravity over a jump (left)

You must keep your weight over the horse's center of gravity by folding forward over a jump. The shoulder, elbow, hip and ankle remain in a straight line.

Closing down the angles

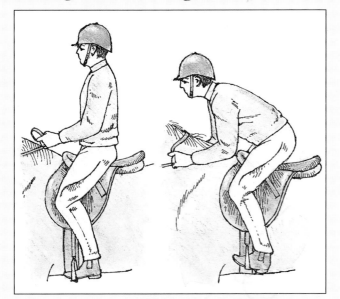

The stirrup leathers are shortened for jumping, closing down the angles at hip, knee and ankle. Think of your body as being a 'W' turned on its side: shoulder to seat, seat to knee, knee to heel, and heel to toe. In the correct jumping position, you flatten the W as much as possible.

A good position

Virginia Leng flattens right down, but does not let her weight get too far forward, as her horse makes a large jump over a gate.

Common faults

Lifting too far out of the saddle

The rider's seat has come too far out of the saddle, causing her legs to straighten and push forwards and her back to round. Her weight is too far back, and she will get behind the horse's movement over the fence.

Being too far forward

The rider has folded too far forward, causing her to hollow her back. As a result, it is impossible for her to keep her leg in the correct position on the girth. The lower leg has moved too far back behind it. She cannot communicate effectively with the horse from this position.

Standing in the stirrups

By standing in her stirrups the rider has opened up the angles at hip, knee and ankle, and raised her hands too high, so making her position in the saddle very insecure.

Pole work

This is a very good exercise for developing rhythm when teaching a horse to jump, or when improving the performance of an older horse. It is also excellent for practicing the correct jumping position.

It is important that you have the distances between the poles correct. A horse will take two strides at the trot to one at the canter. If you have the poles double-spaced, that is, correct for the canter, they will be correct for the trot as well, and you will not need to keep dismounting to move them each time you change gait.

The distance between the poles will depend on your horse's size and stride. The table gives a guide to distances.

When the horse is happy going over one pole, move up to three poles or more. Do not work over just two poles as it might encourage the horse to jump both poles together.

Begin by walking over the poles, and then go over them at a rising trot. Cantering to poles should not be attempted unless the horse has mastered them at the trot. In canter, the horse should just bounce along without taking any steps between the poles.

Distances for pole work

size of horse	length of stride trot	length of stride canter
14½ hh	4 ft	8 ft
	1.2 m	2.4 m
16 hh	4½ ft	9 ft
	1.4 m	2.75 m

Trotting over poles

The rider's position is good. Her weight is slightly forward, her hands are in contact with the horse's mouth, she is sitting down in the saddle and squeezing the horse forwards with her lower legs.

Cantering over poles

The rider has folded forward, closing the angles. Her lower legs are on the girth, and are maintaining a good contact with the horse. Her body is forward, and as she is not leaning on her hands, they are in active contact with the horse's mouth. She is driving the horse on with her lower legs.

Common faults: trotting

Legs too far forward

The rider's leg is too far forward and has straightened, and her back has rounded. This often happens when the horse rushes the poles.

Legs too far back

The rider approaches the poles with her legs too far back along the horse's side, and using the reins to balance. She cannot give the horse precise instructions from this position, and the horse is showing its concern at the lack of communication from the rider by raising its head and hollowing its outline.

Resting on hands

The rider is resting her weight on her hands, and is not making use of the horse's impulsion which she is trying to create with her legs. The horse is not taking a full stride as it approaches the poles.

Common faults: cantering

Position collapsed

Although the rider's leg is in the correct position, her body is collapsing forwards and to one side. She is leaning on her hands and looking down. As a result, the horse's movement is restricted.

Position too upright

The rider is sitting too upright, which puts her weight too far behind the horse's movement. The horse's balance and judgement are adversely affected, and it does not stride cleanly over the poles. Instead, its forefeet are either side of the pole.

Poles leading to a small jump

Once the horse is working well over poles, you can add a small jump at the end of the poles. Use three or four poles on the ground leading to the jump, spaced as before. The last pole should be 2.75 m (9 ft) in front of the jump. Crosspoles are the best type of jump to use as they will help to guide you towards the center of the fence. They will also encourage the horse to make the correct shape over the jump (see page 116).

Jumping exercises over this type of grid teach the horse to approach a fence in a rhythmic canter, the aim being to take the fence in that same rhythm.

Sophie Martindale

Sophie Martindale on Proven Best at Badminton, 1986. Practice over grids and low fences develops a good secure seat, which is the basis of all future jumping work, whether you eventually want to specialize in show-jumping or eventing.

Taking the poles and jump

1 The horse is approaching on a good stride and is looking intently at the fence. The rider is keeping a good conversation going with the horse via her lower legs.

2 The rider is closing down the angles at her hip, knee and ankle as she prepares for the moment of take off. The horse is reacting to her positive instructions by coming into the jump with impulsion and looking alert.

Common faults

Lack of communication

1 The rider stands in her stirrups and keeps her body upright, reducing her chance of communicating properly with the horse. Her hands are too high, and the horse is on too long a rein.

2 The rider's lack of positive signals is causing the horse to lose impulsion. Its back feet are trailing behind and it does not look committed to jump·

3 The horse tackles the jump, but its ears are back, its outline is hollow, and it is taking off unevenly from its hocks.

Weak jumping position (left)

The rider is standing in her stirrups, straightening her body. She is keeping her balance by bracing her hands against the horse's neck. Her whole position is weak and insecure. If the horse chose to swerve out or stop, she would find it very difficult to counteract such misbehaviour.

3 The rider has folded her body down well and is looking straight ahead.

The horse has its weight over its hocks and is beginning to lift its forelegs.

4 The horse takes the fence in its stride.

Individual fences

As you gain confidence through working on grids of poles with a small fence, you can move on to tackle larger, individual fences.

When practicing over larger fences you should retain the last pole on the ground in front of the fence to act as a placing pole. It will bring the horse to the fence in the correct spot for take off.

In order to approach a fence correctly you need to concentrate on establishing a good rhythmic canter with plenty of impulsion, and should wait for the fence to come to you. As with the previous exercise, you should maintain the same rhythmic stride throughout the approach and the jump itself. You should not need to check the horse as you approach the fence.

Present the horse to the fence with your legs wrapped around it. Try to have your lower calf and ankle in contact with the horse's sides, applying a steady pressure to tell the horse that you want it to keep going. If the horse is confident that you will allow its movement with your hands, it will jump without your needing to force or yank it into the air. Keep your body relaxed and stay in balance with the horse over the jump.

If the horse does not give a good jump, it could be for a variety of reasons. The placing pole could be at the wrong distance from the jump, bringing the horse in incorrectly, so check that you have it in the right place. It could be that the horse has had a bad experience in the past. Or it could be that the horse lacks confidence in its rider. As with other riding problems, always ask yourself if you are doing everything correctly.

Good position

The rider (top) is balanced well over the horse. She has folded her body right down. Her lower leg and ankle are wrapped around the horse, and are staying in position in the region of the girth. Her hands have moved forward to allow the horse to stretch out its head and neck over the fence.

Anticipating the fence

The rider (above) has stood up in her stirrups before reaching the fence, and is unable to use her legs correctly. At the same time she has dropped the contact through the reins. A horse might well take advantage of this lack of contact to refuse the fence.

Katharine Burdsall (above)

Practice over grids and small fences is the best preparation for the larger jumps that you meet in the ring.

Nick Skelton (left)

In competition each fence presents a new challenge, designed to test a different aspect of a horse's jumping ability.

Common faults

1

Getting left behind

1 It is easy to get left behind over a jump. The horse may surprise you by taking off early, or it may make a bigger jump than you expect it to.

2

2 The rider copes by slipping the reins, that is, letting them run through her fingers, so that the horse is not restricted at all as it puts in a large jump. This will ensure that she does not catch the horse in the mouth.

Looking down

By looking down and to one side of the horse, the rider is putting herself off balance, and has allowed her leg to move back so that her leg aid will be less effective. As she is looking down, she will be unable to give instructions on landing.

Jumping doubles

When you have negotiated poles and different types of individual fences, you can move on to doubles. These consist of two fences positioned close together, usually with one non-jumping stride in the middle. As you have to negotiate two fences within a short space of time it is even more important that you maintain the correct position, so that you can communicate effectively and positively with the horse throughout the whole jump.

As you approach a double, aim your horse at the center of the fences and look to the second part. This will stop you looking down or to one side as you go over the first part.

You have to judge the correct amount of impulsion carefully coming in to a double. If you ride in with too much impulsion your horse will jump too far in over the first part, and find it difficult to jump out over the second part. On the other hand, if you let your horse crawl over the first element you will be leaving it with too much to do to get out of the combination neatly. In either case, the horse may respond by running out at the second element.

If the combination consists of a spread in and an upright out, it will be more difficult to jump because the spread will encourage the horse to jump big, and it may not be able to collect itself and shorten its stride enough to jump clear over the upright.

When you are building practice fences, bear in mind that if the first element consists of crosspoles, it will help you to come in right and set you up well for the second element.

Anne Kursinski

Anne Kursinski on Starman takes off over the second element of a double at Hickstead, 1987.

Jumping a double

1 The rider's lower leg is on the girth, and her body is folded forward. Her hands are maintaining a good contact with the horse's mouth.

2 The rider is ready to push the horse on using her lower legs. You must not rest on your hands as you come over the first part of a double, or you will not be ready to correct any steering problems ready for the second part.

3 The rider's legs are on the girth, applying pressure to give the horse precise instructions on approaching the second element. There is no hesitation on the horse's part as it prepares for the spread.

4 The crosspoles at the second element help guide the horse to the center of the fence, and it jumps well lifting its shoulders and tucking its forelegs up neatly. The rider is still looking ahead.

5 The rider has folded forward, her lower leg has stayed in position, and she is looking ahead. Her hands are relaxed but in contact, allowing the horse the freedom to use its head and neck as it jumps.

Common faults

Weight too far forward

In pushing on to the second part of the double, the rider is leaning too far forwards, and her seat is coming out of the saddle. In this position she will find it difficult to give precise instructions to the horse as they come in to the second element.

LEISURE RIDING

Leisure riding provides the opportunity to explore a limitless range of different types of terrain and conditions. It can be the most exciting and pleasurable of all forms of horse-riding, not the least because it constantly presents horse and rider with new or unexpected situations and conditions.

The freedom of trail-riding in the mountains or hacking out through unspoilt countryside may seem a far cry from the discipline of the schooling arena. However, the fitness, control, balance and good communication between horse and rider that are developed by training for the competitive disciplines will be invaluable in tackling difficult or unexpected situations. Whether you are riding up and down steep slopes, picking a way across difficult terrain, going through water, or tackling natural obstacles like logs and ditches, you will be able to do so confidently if you have done some basic training. And if necessary you will be able to get the best out of the most sluggish hired horse, and control a difficult or unfamiliar one.

Mountain trail riding

This spectacular riding country in the Rocky Mountains provides the challenge of up- and downhill work as well as tricky river crossings. Good basic horsemanship is essential if you are to get the most out of riding in this type of terrain.

Sun, sea and sand

This thrilling setting in the exotic surroundings provided by Chukka Cove, Jamaica, makes for conditions that encourage horses and riders to let themselves go.

Riding in snow

Horses and riders enjoying the exhilarating experience of riding in the snow in St Moritz. Confidence in your riding skills enables you to enjoy yourself whatever the conditions.

Relaxing after a lesson

A ride across open country provides a good opportunity for horses and riders to relax after the hard work and discipline of formal schooling. These riders are going confidently across flooded ground.

Trail riding: 1

Riding within the confines of a schooling arena, whether it is inside or out, is totally different to cantering across vast open spaces such as fields, pastures or plains. Hills, uneven terrain, roads and gates can all pose problems.

The freedom of an unconfined space can stimulate an otherwise easily controllable horse. It may change from being quite easy to slow down or stop, to being headstrong and difficult. If you ride in company a race can develop, and everyone may become carried away. It is important for your own safety and that of others that you know how to bring your horse back under control.

Most riders have to do some roadwork with their horses so it is vital to know how your horse reacts in traffic. If it is a new horse you should know from the previous owners whether it is traffic-proof, and what is likely to frighten it.

Do not venture onto the roads on a strange horse on your own. Ask a friend with a safe, experienced horse to accompany you and stick to quieter roads at first.

Another way to accustom your horse to traffic is by turning it out in a field close to a major road, if that is possible.

You should seek the help of an experienced person if you need to traffic-proof your horse.

Even the most experienced horse can be suddenly spooked by something on the road. It is therefore vital when doing roadwork to ride properly at all times so that you and your horse remain alert. Never daydream.

You should always wear protective headgear, know your highway code, and be courteous to considerate drivers and other road-users.

Roadwork (above)

Roadwork is a good way of getting your horse fit. You should make sure it is accustomed to traffic before going out on your own.

Exercising (below)

Allow time for exercising across open country in your routine. It helps to keep a horse fresh and prevents it from becoming bored.

Opening and closing a gate

1 Position your horse parallel to the gate with its head facing the latch. take the reins and whip in one hand and with the hand nearest the gate, undo the latch.

2 Use your leg nearest the gate to ask the horse to move away from it (the horse will be turning on its forehand).

3 Open the gate far enough for you to pass through, remembering that some horses become upset and try to rush. If you do not give yourself enough room you could get badly knocked against the gatepost, or unseated.

4 Once through, position the horse parallel to the gate again so that you can pull the gate to, and fasten the latch. Always watch where your horse's head is – a horse can quite easily catch its bridle on a gate latch.

Trail riding : 2

When riding uphill, make sure that your weight is well forward and over your knees so that the horse's back is not carrying your weight but is free to move. Hold on to the mane if necessary to balance yourself, but do not lean on the horse's neck or use the reins to balance. The horse needs its head and neck free in order to balance itself.

When going down a steep hill, always take the direct route. Do not zig-zag down as the horse could easily lose its footing and slip. Sit tall in the saddle, without leaning backwards or forwards, and take your weight down through your legs and heels. Again, the horse must have the freedom to balance itself using its head and neck, but do not let the reins lose contact completely.

Hillwork (above)

Hillwork is beneficial for improving the horse's strength and endurance whatever area of competition you are involved in. Uphill work is of particular value.

Uphill canter (below)

When riding uphill it is important to keep your weight well forward so as to allow the horse maximum freedom of movement.

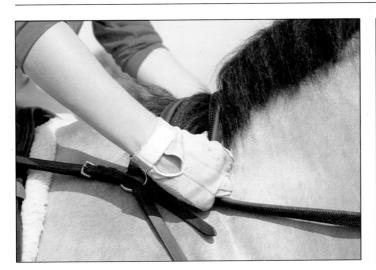

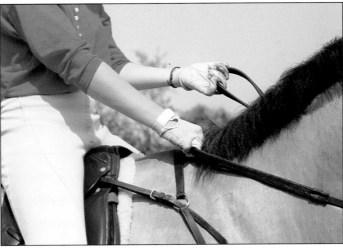

Bridging the reins

If you find that your horse becomes rather strong, you will be able to control it better if you bridge the reins by bracing them against the withers. If the horse pulls, it will be pulling against itself, and cannot pull the reins out of your hands.

Short, sharp tugs

If your horse is going faster than you are happy with, and your position in the saddle is relatively stable, you can slow it down by anchoring one hand in the horse's mane, and giving a series of short sharp tugs with the other rein. If you pull continuously against a horse, it will only pull harder against you.

Relaxation

Horses always enjoy the opportunity to relax that riding out provides, whatever the conditions.

SECTION

3

COMPETITIVE RIDING

SHOW-JUMPING
·
DRESSAGE
·
EVENTING

Expert advisers Roland Fernyhough, Tanya Larrigan-Robinson and Jane Holderness-Roddam give their expert advice on how to improve your riding technique and the horse's performance in the three main competitive areas of show-jumping, dressage and eventing.

Roland Fernyhough

Roland Fernyhough is a former member of the British Olympic team. He now concentrates on training young riders.

Tanya Larrigan-Robinson

Originally born into a circus family, Tanya Larrigan-Robinson has become an internationally known dressage rider, and a former member of the British team in the World Championships. Tanya's training skills are recognized world-wide. She regularly travels to the USA and Australia to teach her methods to up-and-coming riders. In addition she is well known for her exhibition riding.

Jane Holderness-Roddam

Jane Holderness-Roddam (formerly Bullen) was a member of the gold-medal winning British team at the Mexico Olympics. She has also won Badminton and Burghley Horse Trials, and a team gold in the European Championships in 1978, and is a former member of the British team at the World Championships. She now works in Britain and America, bringing on young horses and running teaching clinics.

SHOW-JUMPING

In a show-jumping competition the course builder tests horse and rider not only with different types of fences – uprights, spreads and combinations – but also with changes of direction and variations in distances between fences. His aim is to build a course that will require the horse to jump as well as it can.

You must understand the importance of maintaining balance, controlling rhythm, communicating effectively, and being aware of what the horse is doing. However, it is the horse who has to jump the fences. Your responsibility is to develop your horse's jumping ability and to prepare it for the tests it will meet in the ring. You should follow a training program that progresses steadily from basic training to practice over different types of fences. Work on the horse's stride over poles on the ground and grids, as this will improve the horse's rhythm and help to overcome the common problems of slowing down on the approach to a fence, and taking off too close. When the horse has developed balance and rhythm, you can then work on technique for the different types of fence.

At the end of the day, do not judge yourself by the number of rosettes you have won; what counts is whether you and the horse have ridden a good round.

Michel Robert (below left)

Michel Robert on Lafayette taking a straightforward wall and poles.

Robert Smith (below right)

Robert Smith and April Sun negotiate the famous Irish bank at Hickstead.

An unorthodox style (above)

Annette Lewis on Tutin. This rider's unorthodox jumping style has not been a bar to success.

A famous partnership (left)

John Whitaker on Next Milton competing at the European Championships, 1989.

Correct equipment

Safety is all-important in equestrian sports, and it is essential that you and your horse are always properly outfitted for jumping, whether in the show-ring or the practice field. In addition, riders have to conform to regulations in dress for different levels of competition.

Riders should always wear an approved hat, complete with chin harness done up.

Use a good-quality jumping saddle over a numnah, and a good girth. Use a bit that your horse goes well in, and which you feel confident you can control it with. You see many varieties of bit in the show-jumping ring, from snaffles to hackamores, but don't be tempted to use gadgetry for the sake of it. If your horse goes well in a snaffle and you can handle it in that, be grateful.

Horses take many knocks and scrapes when jumping, so always use tendon boots and fetlock boots. Many people use over-reach boots on the front legs in addition to tendon boots, but they can interfere with the horse's action. It may even step on the back of an over-reach boot if it's a little long.

The World Championships

The US team at Aachen, 1986.

Correct dress

Correct dress depends on the level of show.

National and international classes: men

Men usually wear red jackets. The chief exceptions are competitors from Eire who wear green.

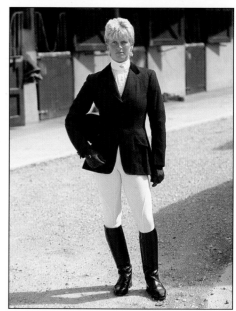

National and international classes: women

Women usually wear a black jacket and either a shirt and collar, or shirt and tie.

Fetlock boots

These protect the horse's legs should it knock into itself.

Protective boots

Tendon boots support the horse's tendons and protect them against strikes from its hind legs.

Draw-reins

Used in conjunction with the rider's aids, draw-reins encourage the horse to hold its head in the correct position: giving from the shoulder onto the reins. They should only be used by an experienced rider, and they should be quite loose, so that they don't restrict the horse's movement, and should never be used to force the horse's head down into the correct position if it isn't ready or able to do this naturally.

Back protection for the horse

A numnah and foam pad protect the horse's back when it is rounding over the fences.

The horse's tack

The horse is wearing a Pelham bit fitted with roundings so that a single rein can be used, a flash noseband, and a running martingale complete with rein stops. A running martingale prevents the horse throwing its head about, but check that it is fitted so that it does not interfere with the horse's head carriage.

Pole work

This exercise, cantering between two poles laid on the ground, is the most important of all exercises for a show-jumper. It forms the basis of all other jumping work because it teaches the horse to approach and take obstacles in one continuous, controlled, rhythmic, rounded movement.

It is natural for a horse to go forwards freely over the flat, but when it sees an obstacle ahead it will begin to hesitate. Poles on the ground will produce the same reaction in you and your horse as if you were jumping a couple of fences, but without any of the risks. The worst that can happen is that the horse will step on one of the poles.

Your aim in doing this exercise is to achieve a controlled, rhythmic stride which the horse can maintain as it goes over a jump. It also helps you to practice seeing a stride, and is good for teaching the horse to lengthen and shorten his stride so as to meet a fence correctly.

You should not take your horse over any fences until you can go over the poles well. If you want, you can replace the poles on the ground with two cross-poles with wings and practice over these before moving on to the next stage of training.

Once you have established a good canter and are happy going over the poles, you can experiment with the stride pattern by asking the horse to put in more or fewer strides.

The perfect shape

The horse goes over the pole in a balanced, active canter. It is making a good round shape with its head, neck, body and legs.

Setting up the poles

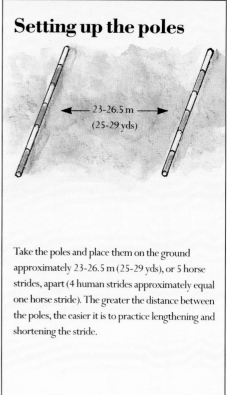

23-26.5 m
(25-29 yds)

Take the poles and place them on the ground approximately 23-26.5 m (25-29 yds), or 5 horse strides, apart (4 human strides approximately equal one horse stride). The greater the distance between the poles, the easier it is to practice lengthening and shortening the stride.

1

Seeing the stride

To help you develop your ability to see the stride, count the number of strides the horse takes between the poles. You can then ask the horse to lengthen and reduce the number of strides it takes or shorten and increase the number of strides.

Shortening the stride

2

A horse can lengthen its stride easily, but shortening and settling back is an unnatural movement that has to be taught and practiced. Squeeze hard with the lower legs, as if trying to slice the horse in half. At the same time, contain the movement with a slight shortening action of the hands. This makes the horse bring its hindquarters well underneath it.

Gridwork

A grid is a series of practice fences set up at related distances, giving the horse a set number of strides between each fence. Gridwork teaches the horse to set itself up right for a fence and to think for itself, as well as increasing its athletic ability. It strengthens the horse and makes it more supple so that it **makes** the correct shape over the jump. In particular, it helps the horse to loosen its shoulders and raise them up over the fence, at the same time arching its neck, dropping its head and folding its forelegs up tight, rounding itself over the fence as it jumps.

You can set up a simple grid consisting of a pole on the ground, the placing-pole, followed by two sets of cross-poles. You should work at the trot until you have developed a good, collected, balanced canter. By trotting over the placing-pole, you ensure that the horse arrives in the correct place to take off for the fence. By arriving consistently in the right place, the horse learns how to set itself up to jump a fence correctly. Whereas if you come in at an uncontrolled canter the horse will be too far off one time, too close in the next. You also do not want to allow the horse to develop the habit of always coming in to fences fast and sailing through them on a long, flat stride.

You can shorten or lengthen the distance between the fences to teach the horse to adjust its stride. If the horse gets into the habit of meeting fences right, it will start to think for itself rather than depending entirely on your instructions. If it lands a bit long it will shorten its stride for the second part; if short, it will lengthen it.

Although gridwork is done mainly for the benefit of the horse, you should practice always maintaining the correct position and riding consistently over the fences.

Correct shape

Aim for this shape over a fence. The hocks are deep to the fence, the shoulders are raised high, the neck is arched, the head dropped, and the front legs are folded up well.

Setting up a grid

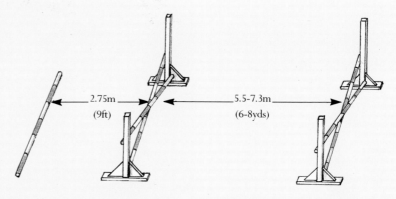

2.75m (9ft)

5.5-7.3m (6-8yds)

A straightforward grid consisting of a placing-pole and two sets of cross-poles. The placing-pole should be positioned about 2.75 m (9 ft) in front of the first fence, and the cross-poles should be 5.5-7.3 m (6-8yd) apart to allow for one stride between them.

After practicing over the cross-poles, you can change the second fence to an upright or a spread, because the horse will always arrive at it in the perfect position to jump it.

Tackling a grid

1 Coming in on a balanced, controlled trot, the horse breaks into a canter over the pole.

2 The rider is in complete control on landing.

3 He increases leg pressure to encourage the horse to lengthen to the second part.

4 The horse lifts it shoulders and rounds well over the second fence.

Common faults

Standing off

The horse has taken off too early. This is making it difficult for it to lift its shoulders and snap up its forelegs neatly.

Uprights

These jumps can take the form of planks, a gate, a single pole between two jump stands, a series of poles one above the other, or a wall. What they all have in common is that they are built vertically to the ground, and have no spread.

They are the easiest fences to have down because they encourage the horse to flatten out rather than to make a good shape, whereas a spread (see page 120) is built in a way that complements the horse's bascule, encouraging it to round over the fence.

To jump an upright successfully, your approach must be balanced and collected, with plenty of impulsion. If anything, you want to come in on a lengthening stride to teach the horse to get in deep and come back on to its hocks, really using its hindquarters to make a very round shape in the air. Allow the horse's movement with your hands and squeeze the horse up into the air with your legs. If the horse stands off, it will have to stretch to get over the fence, thereby losing the correct, rounded shape. Jump like this regularly, and the horse will get into the habit of jumping flat.

When practicing over verticals, always get in close so that the horse learns to round over them properly. When riding in competition,

give the horse a little more room so that it can take the jump in its natural stride but still make a good shape. This will be easier for it, and may also save valuable seconds in a jump-off. However, don't stand off so far that the horse jumps long and flat.

Verticals are particularly tricky when they come at the end of a course. Horse and rider are eager to finish, and may have been pushing on hard over previous fences, so

there is a great temptation to rush them. Be particularly careful to control your approach in this situation so that you jump clear.

Jumping uprights

Rob Ehrens (left) clearing a typical upright on Olympic Sunrise at the Horse of the Year Show, 1987. Lisa Jacquin (above) on For the Moment in Paris, 1987.

Jumping an upright

1 By applying pressure with the legs, the rider has the horse coming in on a lengthening but collected stride, and getting deep into the fence. Its hindquarters are positioned well underneath it to get the necessary upward and forward thrust.

2 The horse has lifted its shoulders well, arched its neck and dropped its head on take-off, and folded up its front legs. The rider has folded forward over the jump. His hands have given, but still maintain contact.

Take-off position

In training, get the horse deep into the fence so that it learns to make a very rounded shape.

In competition, give it a little more room so that it can take the jump in its natural stride.

If you take-off too early, the horse will flatten out over the fence and risk having it down.

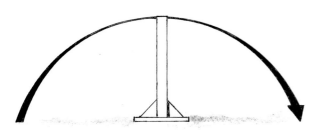

Common faults

Standing off

1 The horse is taking off too early. It is having to reach for the fence, and its front legs are dangling.

3 The horse is coming down too early. It is dropping its shoulders, raising its head and hollowing its back in trying to clear the fence.

2 The horse is at its maximum height, but not over the top of the upright.

3 As the horse prepares to land it maintains its rounded shape. Notice that the rider's leg stays in the same position, applying pressure behind the girth, throughout the jump.

Spreads

Spread fences have width as well as height. They include parallel bars, triple bars, oxers and a wall with rails behind. Fences that slope up away from you are easier to jump than true parallels. For any spread, the horse has to jump wide and high, yet the wider a horse jumps the less easily it can achieve height.

In order to gain optimum height as well as width, over a spread the horse must get deep into the fence on take off and bring its hocks well underneath it. If it stands off, it will clip the top.

You should approach the fence on a deep, lengthening stride. Accurate jumping is essential over this type of fence. You need to be able to see the stride, because the horse must have room to lengthen into the fence. It must not be shortening its stride at the last minute in order to get close to the rail. This ability to see the stride marks out a good ride. It cannot be taught, although it can be developed by practice over poles (see page 114).

If the horse is supple from flatwork and jumping exercises over grids (see page 116), it will be able to get its hindquarters right in underneath it, bringing its hocks close to the front rail. From this position it springs out over the fence in a good round shape.

You can get away with standing too far off a parallel only if the fence is not very wide or high – or if your horse is a brilliant jumper. Do not try to train over large fences. Set up a simple, small parallel spread and practice jumping it perfectly.

The correct shape

The width of the horse's jump is measured from the point where its hocks take off to the point where its front feet land. It should make an arc over the fence, the highest point of which must be over the highest part of the fence.

Jumping a spread

1 The rider has judged the approach accurately. The horse's hocks are well underneath it and close in to the front rail. The rider applies the leg continuously to maintain balance and impulsion.

2 The horse is centrally positioned as it reaches optimum height at the top of the parallel.

The correct shape over a spread

The horse has come up strongly off its hocks. It is lifting its shoulders up over the fence and is rounding well. A horse needs to be very supple in the shoulders in order to jump spreads well.

Taking off too early

1 The rider has asked the horse to take off too soon, and its forelegs are not folding up neatly.

2 The horse is beginning its descent while it is still over the top of the fence, and is flattening out.

3 The horse lands in balance the same distance beyond the fence as it took off in front of it.

Combination fences: doubles

Combinations are difficult to jump because, when faced with a line of fences, riders tend to panic, which in turn makes the horse panic. As a result they rush at the fence, making it more difficult to come to it correctly. As they go over the first element, they are worrying about the second. The horse raises its head to look at it before landing over the first, causing it to flatten out over the first part at the risk of having it down.

It is up to you to steady your horse and keep its concentration fixed on the element you are jumping until you have landed over it.

Always jump combinations one fence at a time. Do not gallop into them, but ride very firmly. Apply pressure with the leg in order to create impulsion, but do not confuse impulsion with speed. You need to apply more pressure and create a stronger rhythm if the first part is a spread than if it is an upright. Work at jumping the first part really well, to keep the horse concentrating and give it confidence.

Your landing should be controlled and balanced. You should not be leaning on your hands, and they should not move on the reins. Recover your position in the saddle immediately. You will then be able to ask for any adjustments to stride or pace in preparation for the next element.

When practicing, concentrate on achieving a rounded, balanced approach, and teach the horse to take the jumps steadily so that it learns to relax. Do not let it rush on just because there is another fence ahead.

Jumping a double

1 Horse and rider have come in on a controlled stride and the horse is arching well over the first element, an upright.

2 The rider is applying pressure with the leg and the horse is lengthening its stride in order to get in close to the second element, a spread.

Good concentration

Neat, controlled jumping, with horse and rider concentrating on the fence in hand. If the elements of a combination are approached in the same way, they should not cause you concern.

Common faults

Lack of concentration

1 The horse has just realized that there is another fence ahead and has raised its head to look at it. As a result it is flattening out as it comes down.

2 The horse lands short over the first element, and has a lot of ground to make up if it is to get close enough in to the parallel.

3 The rider is right forward and is really having to push the horse on to reach the second element. They risk standing too far off from it and landing in the middle.

Combination fences: trebles

Exactly the same approach applies to trebles as to doubles. Jump the first element as if it were a single fence. When you land over it, put pressure on with the leg if you need to lengthen to the next element, contain with the hands if you need to shorten. Whether the second part is a spread or an upright, meet it like an individual fence. Once over it, do whatever is needed in order to meet the third element correctly.

Accurate and balanced riding are more important than ever with a treble. And remember that the faster your approach, the more likely you are to have problems because the horse will not be able to set itself up right for the different types of fence in the combination.

As with all practice jumping, keep the fences small and build up the horse's confidence gradually.

An imposing treble

This treble, with its complicated pattern of poles, will need very accurate jumping.

Jumping a treble

1 The horse takes off well over the first element, a vertical. The rider's lower leg is squeezing the horse into the air, his hands give with the movement, but they are still in contact with the horse's mouth.

2 Horse and rider are balanced and controlled on landing. The rider sits down in the saddle and applies pressure with the legs to encourage the horse to lengthen into the second element, a spread.

Running out

1 The horse is surprised on seeing a third element to jump, and the idea of running out has just occurred to it. It is moving to the right and twisting its body, while the rider is pulling it to the left to try to keep it straight on to the fence.

2 To correct this, the rider sits down in the saddle, and rides with a strong outside leg, so that the horse is in no doubt that it is going to jump the fence.

3 The spread has been cleared, and the rider is applying pressure with his legs and containing the movement with his hands in order to meet the third element, another vertical, on a shorter stride.

4 The horse has brought its hindquarters underneath it and rounds well over the vertical.

Spooky fences

Fences with water or ditches under them, fluttering flags, brightly painted poles or planks, or odd colors, can all spook a horse, making it hesitant about jumping them. Very narrow fences, and ones that have little filling-in material, may also worry a horse.

When taking this type of fence, don't make the mistake of galloping at it in the belief that the faster you go, the more likely you are to clear it. If you are approaching at speed, the horse is far more likely to take fright and back off at the last moment when it sees what it is being asked to jump.

The correct approach is to come in at a slow pace so that the horse can see where you are pointing it and take a good look at what's coming. At the same time squeeze hard with the legs to create plenty of impulsion and give it confidence.

It is better to come in at a trot and 'pop' the fence, than to come galloping in.

As long as the horse is not frightened by these kinds of fences, he will learn to trust you and respond to your instructions. Construct small versions of some of these fences at home to get your horse used to taking unusual-looking jumps. For example, you can put a white board on the ground underneath a simple upright to simulate a water tray.

Jumping a water tray

1 On the approach the rider is pushing the horse on in a firm but controlled manner, squeezing with the legs to reassure the horse.

2 The horse is a little concerned, but is picking itself up well.

3 The horse has been given confidence by the rider's positive approach and it makes the optimum shape with its shoulders over the fence.

Common faults

Backing off

1 The horse's approach is unsure and hesitant. The rider is having to increase the pressure quietly with his legs to persuade the horse to take the fence.

2 The horse's position as it takes off is crouched and tense, with its hindquarters close to the floor.

Spooky fences

Water jump (right)

You should prepare your horse for water jumps before meeting them in the ring. When training your horse to jump water, start with a small, inviting jump and increase the width gradually. Do not gallop at this type of fence, but approach it with plenty of impulsion to encourage the horse to stretch out over it.

A distracting upright (below)

However distracting the "spooky" element of a fence, concentrate on jumping the fence itself correctly.

Good preparation (right)

A good way to prepare your horse for a fence that incorporates water or a ditch is to use a piece of board painted white or blue under a practice fence. Once the horse has learnt that there is nothing to be frightened about, you need not be concerned when you come across this type of fence in the ring.

The high wall (left)

It is not just the height of the wall that makes it spooky. Because it is solid, the horse cannot see what is beyond and may therefore be reluctant to jump it. It requires determined, accurate riding and plenty of impulsion, as well as exceptional jumping ability. This horse has not approached with enough impulsion, and has decided not to attempt it.

An exotic challenge (below)

A fence like this should be treated like any other upright fence but approached with very firm riding in order to give the horse confidence.

A spread in disguise (above)

Elaborate decorations often disguise a relatively easy fence, as here where giant arrangements of flowers surround a straightforward spread.

Walking a course

Walking the course is an essential part of preparation for the ring, not only to memorize the sequence of jumps, but to plan out how to ride them.

Walk the course as you will ride it, remembering that you should use as much of the ring as possible, except when you are jumping off against the clock. Work out the number of strides you will have coming in to awkward fences and those that are close together.

In particular, you need to assess the distances in any combinations. To do this accurately, you need to know the length of your own stride, and the length of your horse's stride. You will also need to decide in advance on the rhythm and pace at which you will ride the jump. You can then work out how many strides you will have between the elements (see page 114).

If you know that you will have to stretch to reach the second or third element, you can push the horse on over the first element so that you land over it with the horse going forwards, and increase pressure with the leg so that he lengthens out. Alternatively, if the distance will be very tight for your horse, you know that you will have to be ready to collect him back after landing.

Pacing the distances (above)

Michael and John Whitaker pace out the distance between fences in order to plan their rounds.

A typical show-jumping course

A show-jumping course will include all types of fences – uprights, spreads, doubles and trebles – in different forms and combinations. When planning your round, choose a line that brings you in straight to each fence and make use of as much of the ring as possible.

Studying the course (above)

Nick Skelton (left) and Pierre Durand take a close look at the course.

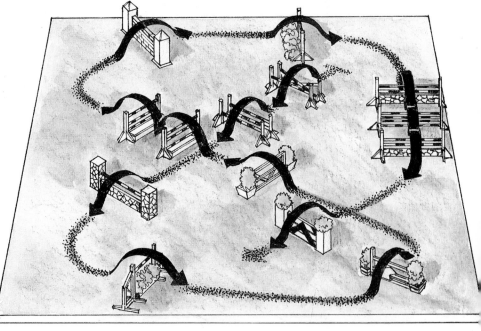

Planning a round

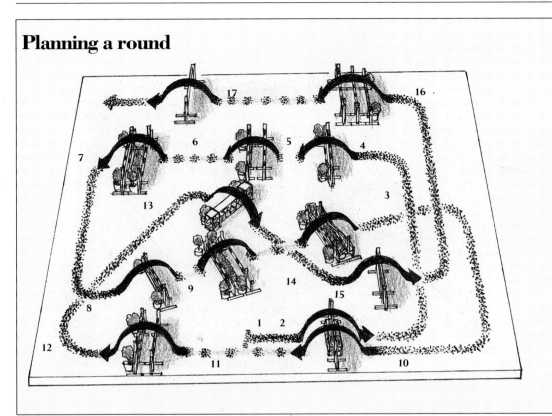

(1) Start on the left rein. (2) This vertical needs a collected approach. (3) Be on the left rein here. (4) The upright first element requires a collected approach. (5) Lengthen the stride for the second element. (6) Pace out the distance between the fences to calculate the number of strides. (7) Lead on the left leg here. (8) Collect for this combination. (9) Apply leg to lengthen the stride. (10) This was also the first fence. (11) Pace out the distance. There may be room to shorten the stride. (12) Keep on the right rein. (13) Be careful to meet the fence straight on after this awkward turn. (14) Make a proper square turn so that the horse has time to see the next fence. (15) The horse may be tired and could flatten out over this vertical. Collect and jump carefully. (16) Approach on a lengthening stride to take off as close as possible. (17) Collect for a steady approach to the last fence.

Walking the course (left)

Riders walking the course at the Royal Show, 1979. It is very important to walk the course carefully in order to plan your round.

Riding a course

It is one thing to jump any amount of single fences, but show-jumping is about completing a course. To do this successfully you need to combine a controlled, rhythmic pace with the ability to execute tight turns and changes of speed and direction smoothly and calmly, at the same time getting the optimum ability out of your horse over the different types of fence. You should aim for a smooth, controlled round, in which all these elements merge into one fluid, balanced performance.

When practicing at home, aim to be able to canter round ten fences in a controlled way, maintaining the same rhythm throughout the round. A horse only has so many jumps in him, so do not ride him over a course too much at home, and do not practice over large fences – keep them for the ring. Alter the type and sequence of the fences from one session to the next to keep you and the horse alert.

When setting up a practice course, incorporate several turns and changes of direction to keep the horse balanced and yourself thinking. Experienced horses will automatically put themselves on the correct leg after jumping a fence. Others, with help from their rider, will perform a flying change. However, don't be afraid to bring your horse back to a trot if you need to in order to change direction. Then ask for canter again with the correct leg leading.

Think about what you ask the horse to do in the ring. For example, do you ask it to approach fences short, at an angle, or on the turn? Then create these problems over little fences at home so that the horse can learn to cope with them without frightening itself.

An unusual course (below)

The bank in the foreground adds an unusual element to this course at Dinard, France.

Training a novice

If you are working a young horse or are new to show-jumping, break the course up into several short sequences of two or three fences ending in a turn or corner. Treat each sequence as a separate round, aiming for perfect balance and rhythm, going back to trot at the end of each sequence and asking the horse to change leg on the turns. This will teach you to maintain rhythm and consistency throughout the round, and to avoid the all-too-frequent mistake of getting gradually faster, flatter and longer as the round progresses.

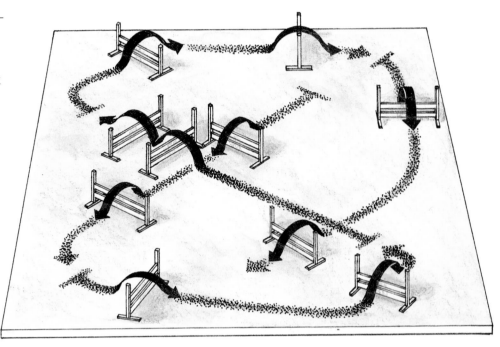

The ultimate goal (below)

The Olympic Stadium, Seoul, 1988.

Riding a course

1 The course begins with an upright. The horse is on the right rein and is being brought in on a bouncy, collected canter, with the aim of maintaining that rhythm throughout the round.

6 The horse is now leading with the left leg. The rider has asked it to change in anticipation of a left turn after the next fence, the water tray.

5 The horse jumps out well over the spread. The rider is well balanced and looking straight ahead.

2 After clearing the first fence, horse and rider begin to make a right-handed turn to the next. Ride the turns smoothly to maintain rhythm and keep the horse balanced.

3 Horse and rider make a fairly wide turn to come in to the parallel bars. There is no need to cut corners unless you are in a jump-off, as long as you keep within the allotted time. The horse is leading with its inside (right) foreleg.

4 The turn has enabled them to meet the parallel with a good central approach, well balanced and getting in close to the front rail.

Sequence continued overleaf

Riding a course

7 The rider pushes the horse on with a straight, positive approach and rhythmical, balanced stride that encourage the horse to jump.

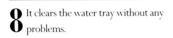

8 It clears the water tray without any problems.

9 After the water tray, they turn on the left rein to approach the double. The horse is nicely balanced, maintaining its rhythm, with the left leg leading.

Leading off on the correct leg

You can teach a young horse to lead off from a jump
on the correct leg for the way you want to turn.
Jump a small fence in a figure-of-eight, coming in at
a slight angle. As you come over the fence, you swing
your body weight in the direction you want to go.
The horse will soon learn to tell from this which way
you are going to turn, and will lead off on the correct
leg on landing.

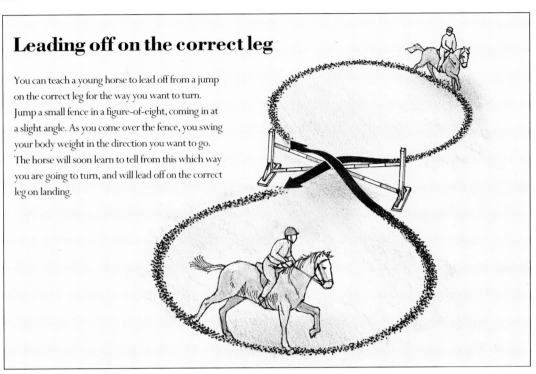

10 They come in towards the
double with a good, straight
approach and at a steady, collected pace.

Sequence continued overleaf

Riding a course

11 The horse stands back a bit at the first element, an upright. The rider applies pressure with the lower leg to encourage it over the fence.

Making a flying change

This movement will be a great help in the ring. Use your outside leg strongly behind the girth to ask the horse to strike off with that outside hind. By doing this it will be leading with the inside foreleg. At the same time, shift your weight to the inside of the saddle in the direction of the bend. With regular practice the horse comes to recognize these aids and will respond by changing its leading leg.

12 It lands well out over the upright, going forwards, and has not been distracted by the second element.

13 The horse has adjusted to meet the parallel correctly, and springs out over it in a good shape.

DRESSAGE

Monica Theodorescu

Monica Theodorescu performing on Ganimedes at the European Championships, 1989. Modern dressage requires the horse to be active and free while still displaying all the qualities of power and speed that are its inherent characteristics.

Robert Dover on Federleight

It takes many years to train a partnership for top-class competition.

D ressage is one of the most skilled forms of riding, and it represents the ultimate in harmony and understanding between horse and rider.

The aim of the dressage test is the execution of a series of reasonably simple movements extremely well. However, it is not enough just to master the content of a dressage test. You must perform it with style and grace if you are to pick up good marks.

In order to achieve this, the horse must be agile, supple and keen; it must be given time to build up the correct muscles and learn the different paces and movements; and it must develop self-carriage. The rider must also undergo a training program that requires dedication and self-discipline.

It takes several years to train a partnership to advanced level. However, it is a sport that you can derive much satisfaction from, whatever level you compete at, as competitions provide a meeting-place where horses and riders can measure their progress through the long years of training.

Sheer elegance (above)

Dressage should create an impression of
sheer elegance and total harmony
between horse and rider.

Competition (left)

Dressage tests give horse and rider the
opportunity to measure their progress
through the years of training.

Clothing and tack

The rules about clothing and tack in a dressage test are strict. You must know what they are because if either you or your horse is incorrectly dressed, you will be liable to a fine and disqualification.

The rider

At Elementary and Novice levels, you must wear cream, beige or white jodhpurs, a white shirt, stock or tie, and a tweed, dark blue or black jacket. You can wear either long or jodhpur boots. An approved riding hat is compulsory and hat covers must be black, brown or navy.

Dress for Medium level tests is the same as for Novice, except that you must wear an approved riding hat instead of a crash hat.

For Advanced level tests, you wear either a tail coat and top hat, or a black or navy-blue coat and bowler. You must wear a white shirt with stock or tie; light-colored gloves; cream, beige or white breeches or jodhpurs; and long boots. Women must wear a hair net.

At Advanced level spurs are worn, but must be made of metal, and the band around the heel must be smooth. The shank must be on the back of the heel, pointing towards the rear. Whips are allowed in most classes and can be any length, but check on the rules beforehand. Excessive use of whips and spurs is not allowed.

The horse

Regulations about the horse's tack must be followed as carefully as those about the rider's clothing and equipment.

For all classes except Advanced, the tack should consist of: an English or Continental saddle, this can be a dressage saddle if you wish; and a snaffle bridle with a cavesson or flash noseband.

For Advanced level tests, the horse wears a double bridle with a cavesson noseband.

The rules apply even when exercising your horse prior to a test. Again, the correct saddle, snaffle or double bridle, and cavesson, dropped or flash noseband must be worn. However, the horse can wear protective boots or leg bandages for warming up, but remember to take them off before you go into the ring.

Novice tests (far left)

A tweed or dark jacket is worn, white shirt, light-colored jodhpurs, stock or tie, long boots and an approved hat.

Medium tests (left)

Dress is the same as for Novice tests but a stock is often worn instead of a tie.

Advanced tests (below)

At Advanced level, a black tail coat and top hat are worn, or dark jacket and bowler. Top hats and bowlers should be worn straight on the head, resting just above the eyebrows. They should not sit on the back of the head.

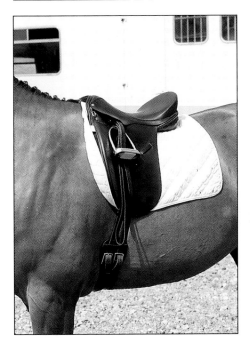

Dressage saddle

The dressage saddle, which has a deep seat and straight-cut flaps, is ideal for riding a test as it is designed to keep the rider in the correct position.

Double bridle

A double bridle is compulsory for Advanced tests, and can also be worn for Medium ones. In the hands of an experienced rider it provides a fine degree of control.

Flash noseband

The flash noseband is a combination of the cavesson and drop nosebands. It is allowed in all classes except Advanced.

Tack that cannot be used in competition

- Western style or brightly colored saddles.

- Grackle and kineton nosebands.

- Martingales.

- Side or running reins.

- Boots (with the exception of equiboots) and leg bandages.

- Blinkers.

Common faults

Kineton noseband

This horse would be disqualified from the dressage arena. It is wearing a kineton noseband, a martingale and protective boots.

Grackle noseband

The grackle noseband is not allowed at any level of dressage test.

Dressage training

The term dressage covers all training done on the flat, and dressage movements and exercises are used for training all horses regardless of which area of the sport they compete in. Its aim is to produce a horse that is strong, supple, well-developed and obedient to its rider.

You have to teach the horse to move at the different gaits, progressing gradually from one to the next. In doing this, you must always take into account the horse's stage of development and training. In the demonstration sequences in this section, most of the movements are shown first by a novice horse that is still learning some of the gaits and then by an advanced horse, to illustrate what can be expected at different stages of a horse's development. The advanced horse also demonstrates the self-carriage that all dressage horses must develop. Build up gradually, as the horse needs to develop the muscles necessary to perform each action. A horse can be ruined if it is asked to do too much too early.

The rider also has to undergo an intensive training program. You have to work on your position in the saddle. You have to learn to use the leg, seat and hand aids independently of each other but correctly balanced for the movement you are executing, so that you control the whole horse all of the time. And you need to learn to work with a relaxed but positive mind, as any tenseness or indecision on your part will instantly communicate themselves to the horse. A young horse should be worked for about a half-hour a day. and you should include hillwork and gridwork in the training routine to get the horse fit and keep its mind fresh. Always remember that your horse is not a machine. Do not drill it, and do not just sit on top and try to dominate it. The horse must want to work with you if you are to get the best out of it.

The perfect setting (right)

Blenheim Palace provides a wonderful backdrop for a dressage competition.

The dressage arena

The smaller-sized arena is used for tests up to Medium level, the larger arena for international events. It is useful to practice in a large arena, especially when you are working on advanced movements. The arena is marked with letters which, in a test, indicate where the movements being performed should begin and end.

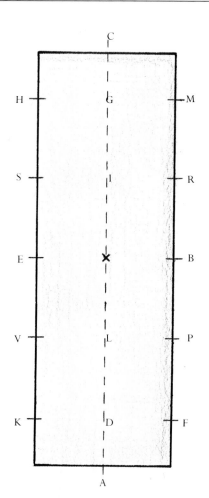

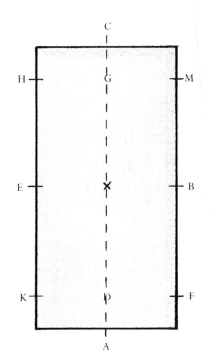

Fizzy horse (left)

If your horse is very lively, you are well advised to turn it out for half an hour, or to lunge it before beginning a schooling session.

Working as one (below)

The aim of dressage training is for horse and rider to learn to work as one.

The walk

In walk, the horse must have good forward movement, be straight, and responsive to your aids. It must be moving forward symmetrically, with the power coming from behind. You must be as still and relaxed as possible and allow with your hands to let the horse take a full stride.

There are four types of walk: free, collected, medium, and extended. The free walk is a walk on a long, loose rein. The horse takes long, easy strides and can relax and stretch out its neck.

In collected walk you are looking for increased flexing in the hocks and activity in the joints to give short, elevated steps. The outline should be shortened, and the hind feet should fall just in, or slightly behind, the prints of the front feet. The collected walk is created by using the half-halt repeatedly while maintaining the gait.

The medium walk comes between free and extended. The horse begins to lengthen and extend its stride and the hind legs slightly overtrack the forelegs. It also begins to lengthen its body although the outline remains compact and rounded overall. Its steps should be free and active, and you should maintain a light contact with the horse's mouth.

In extended walk the horse must just release the outline and become longer and lower. It must cover as much ground as possible with each stride while maintaining regular steps. You ask for the extended walk by increasing the pressure from your seat and closing your legs against the horse. At the same time you allow the horse to stretch its neck forward and take the rein.

Free walk: novice (top)

The rider has given the horse the freedom to lower and stretch out its head and neck.

Collected walk: novice (above)

The rider is using her legs to create more activity in the hindquarters, at the same time using a series of half-halts to ask the horse to shorten and heighten its stride.

Medium walk: novice (top)

By using her legs and seat the rider asks the horse to lengthen its stride a little. She has a light contact with her hands. The horse's outline remains rounded.

Extended walk: novice (above)

The rider is closing her lower legs to ask the horse to stretch out and lengthen its stride, and allows it to take the rein as it does so. In extending its body, this horse has flattened out too much.

Medium walk: advanced horse

This horse has a shorter stride than the younger one. It needs to drop its neck a fraction and lengthen out.

Extended walk: advanced horse

The horse's hind leg is coming through well from behind and is overtracking the print left by the front foot. Again, it needs to drop a little lower in the neck and lengthen out. Then its hind leg would come through further, lengthening its stride.

The trot: working and collected

In trot you should aim for free, active, regular steps, and a general impression of elasticity and suppleness, with the hind legs engaged. It is a difficult gait to do correctly, and young horses particularly tend to hurry, throwing themselves and their riders off-balance.

There are four types of trot: working, collected, medium and extended. You must be able to follow the movement of extended and collected trot very closely. If your seat is not deep enough, the rhythm of the pace will probably be lost.

The working trot is used for horses that are not ready to learn collection. It demonstrates whether the horse is properly balanced, has good hock action, and is on the bit.

As with all collected gaits, collected trot requires plenty of impulsion coming from the hindquarters. You then contain the energy with the half-halt as it comes through from behind, to create springy, elevated gaits. The horse's hind legs should be very active, with increased flexion in the hocks, so that they come well under the horse.

The horse's ability in collected trot will depend to a certain extent on its conformation and natural action, as well as its stage of development. Some horses have a very round natural trot action, and can achieve the required flexion up and hold more easily than others. A horse that has a straight, flat action will have difficulty achieving the same degree of flexion and roundness.

Working trot (above)

The horse is attentive, it has a good outline and a nice length of stride.

Correct rising trot (left)

The rider has her feet lightly balanced in the stirrups, and her lower legs are wrapped around the horse's body. She is relaxed and independent of her hands, and rises with the horse's movement.

Incorrect rising trot (left)

The rider's body is stiff, and she is leaning slightly backwards. Her hands are raised, and the reins are too long, so she has lost the contact.

Towards collection: novice horse (top)

The horse has good flexion in the hock, and is coming up in front. It is beginning to make its stride shorter and more active and its outline rounder.

Collected trot: advanced horse (above)

The rider is asking for impulsion and using the half-halt to create a very elevated collected trot. The horse is flexing well and moving with a rounded action.

Common faults

Horse on the forehand

The stride is shorter but the horse has too much weight on its forehand. The rider is slightly forward, and looks as if she is trying to carry it. She needs to sit upright and half-halt to sit the horse down and release and lighten the front.

Resistance

The horse is arguing with the bit. The rider is asking it to start to collect, and is possibly using too much hand, as opposed to using her back and seat properly to ask for the gait. She needs to sit up straight and push the horse forwards.

The trot: medium and extended

Medium trot comes between working and extended in length of stride. There should be plenty of impulsion from the hindquarters, and the horse should be taking energetic strides. Its neck should be slightly extended. The horse must be over-tracking, and the stride must be of equal length in front and behind. Uneven strides show that the horse is not working actively behind.

In extended trot the horse lengthens its outline to the maximum to produce long strides. Prepare for the extended trot with the half-halt. Then give strong aids, pushing with the seat and closing the legs firmly against the horse, and release the movement through the reins. Go with the stride as you ask for it. If you do not go with the movement, you will get behind it and end up pulling on the reins.

Medium trot: novice horse (above)

The rider is asking for a lengthened stride with her seat and legs and is keeping a light contact with her hands. The horse is working actively and the strides in front and behind are of equal length.

Medium trot: advanced horse (left)

The rider is fractionally behind the horse's movement. However, as she went with the movement she is not interfering with the horse's stride.

Lack of preparation

The horse has its head up, is resisting the bit and going onto the forehand. It is "running" and the rider is having to balance it with her hands. In asking for the gait, she should have used her legs more to engage the horse's hindquarters and push it forward, and then allowed the movement with her hands.

Extended trot: novice horse (above)

The length of stride is good. The horse is still learning this gait, and is going into it too much, with its weight on the forehand. The rider is leaning fractionally forward in an attempt to help it. However, she is allowing the movement to come through. The pace is very active, but a little unbalanced.

Extended trot: advanced horse (right)

The rider has asked for the gait by preparing the horse with a half-halt, pushing the horse on strongly, and then releasing the forward movement with her hands, keeping a light contact with the horse's mouth. The horse is responding with a smooth, active extended stride. You can see how much it has lengthened compared with the medium trot.

The canter

In canter you are aiming for a general impression of regular steps, lightness, roundness, and acceptance of the bit. The horse should be light in the forehand so that its shoulders are free and mobile, and it should demonstrate good hock action. The horse's back should be round and swinging, and you should be relaxed in the saddle, absorbing the movement. In addition, you must keep the horse going straight, that is with the inner hind foot in line with the inner front foot.

The four canter paces are: working, collected, medium and extended.

The working canter is used for horses who are not ready to learn collection. It demonstrates a free, balanced gait.

Collected canter should have a clear 3-time beat. The horse should be on the bit, moving forward with its neck raised and arched. It should bring its hindquarters well underneath it, shifting its weight back and lightening its forehand to produce short, springy strides.

In medium canter, again the 3-time movement should be well marked. The horse should lengthen a little, and its hind leg should come well under its body, producing an active stride.

In extended canter the hind leg should come well under the horse's body in order to lengthen the stride as much as possible and produce a longer outline. However, apply the pushing aids gently so that the horse does not go forward in a series of jerks. Extended canter is a difficult gait to maintain because the horse has a natural inclination to rush its strides rather than lengthen them.

It can be difficult to keep a horse straight in canter. If you find this a problem, you should first think about your own position. If you are not sitting square in the saddle you will make the horse go crooked. Next, think about the aids you are giving. If you are not balancing them correctly, the horse will not go straight. For example, if your outside leg is too far back, it can make the horse's quarters swing in. If your inside hand is too strong, creating too much bend in the horse's neck, you will lose control of the shoulders and the outside shoulder will fall to the outside.

Starting collection: novice horse (top)

The horse is starting collection. Its neck is raised, its hindquarters are rounded and lowered, and it is starting to sit. The rider is slightly against the horse, twisting and pulling back on the inside rein.

Extended canter: novice horse (above)

The rider is in a good position, and the horse is achieving a good stride. It is on the forehand a little because its hindquarters are not quite engaged enough. Although it is lengthening well, it should not drop its head, but must remain in self-carriage as the advanced horse has done.

Collected canter: advanced horse (above left)

The horse's outline is shortened and rounded. In the middle of a stride it is like a coiled spring ready to unwind.

Medium canter: advanced horse (centre left)

The stride is a little shorter than the extended canter below. The rider has just gone forward with the movement of the horse. She is using her legs to push the horse on and has a good position in the saddle.

Extended canter: advanced horse (below left)

The horse is making a good long stride, but it is a little flat behind the saddle. It needs to engage the hindquarters more by bringing the inside leg a little further under its body.

Common faults

A flat outline

The horse is not using its hindquarters actively enough, with the result that they are not properly rounded. This can be seen behind the saddle, where it is flatter than in the picture above.

Resistance to the rider

The horse is on the forehand, resisting the rider. She needs to use her legs to increase the activity in the horse's hindquarters.

Transitions: 1

Transitions between gaits and within each gait, for example from collected trot to extended trot, should be executed smoothly and positively, with plenty of impulsion. A rough transition shows poor preparation and lack of balance.

The key to riding a good transition is to have the horse attentive and listening to the aids, and to give a clear, well-prepared request to change gait.

A good way to improve the quality of your transitions is to count the strides as you practise. Ride on a circle, counting the number of strides that you do at each gait and changing the pace on the same count each time. For example, do 10 strides in trot, 10 strides in canter, 10 strides in trot, 10 strides in canter. This will make the horse listen to you. It will also teach you to prepare in advance, because you know that you have to make the transition on the count of 10 each time.

Walk to trot

1 The rider is preparing the horse to go forward into trot. She is pushing the horse on with her seat and legs and shortening the reins, and the horse is becoming rounder.

2 The horse moves smoothly into trot. The rider goes with the horse into the new gait, so it is not having to move forward against her hand.

Lack of preparation

1 The rider is not doing anything to prepare the horse. It is on a long rein and is resisting slightly.

2 As a result, it has taken off into trot and hollowed its outline. The rider has not gone with the movement so is pulling back on the bit.

Trot to walk (far left)

The rider has sat down in the saddle, closed her lower leg against the horse and contained with her hands to ask for the transition. She goes with the horse as it moves into walk.

Bad preparation (left)

The rider is almost standing in the saddle, and is pulling back on the reins with her hands raised. In response the horse has raised its head, hollowed, and is resisting her.

Trot to canter

1 The rider feels the inside rein to give slight flexion to the leg she wants leading – in this case the right (inside) leg. Her outside leg goes back behind the girth.

2 The inside leg comes well forward under the horse and the rider moves with the horse as they go smoothly into canter.

Canter to trot (top)

The rider has sat down in the saddle and asked for the transition down to trot using her legs while squeezing with her hands to check the movement.

Lack of preparation (above)

The rider has failed to prepare for the transition, and the horse is on its forehand, almost falling into the new gait. She should have used the half-halt before asking for the transition.

Transitions: 2

The canter to walk transition shown here is the most difficult transition to perform. The horse must be listening to the rider and engaging its hindquarters in preparation for the transition. If it is not engaged enough, it will hollow, bringing up its head and neck, and will fall back against the rider.

Canter to walk: novice horse

1 The rider has not prepared for the transition, and the horse has its weight on the forehand. Because the horse is a little unbalanced, horse and rider are pulling against each other.

2 The rider is having to use too much hand to bring the horse back into walk. The horse is not submitting to this pressure, but is pulling back to try to escape it.

3 The horse falls into walk, with its weight on the forehand. It is against the movement all the way through.

Canter to walk: advanced horse

1 The horse is balanced and collected, with its hind legs coming well underneath it.

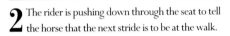

2 The rider is pushing down through the seat to tell the horse that the next stride is to be at the walk.

3 The horse moves into walk with its weight well back on its hindquarters.

Turn on the forehand

The turn on the forehand is used in the early part of a horse's training. It increases the horse's suppleness, and teaches it to be obedient to the rider's aids. The movement is also valuable in teaching the rider to control the whole horse.

You ask the horse to fix its shoulders, and using your leg on the girth you push the horse's hindquarters round. The horse's hind legs step across each other so that it pivots on its forehand.

The turn on the forehand is done from a standstill. Move in a little way from the side of the arena so that the horse has enough space to turn in.

How the horse turns

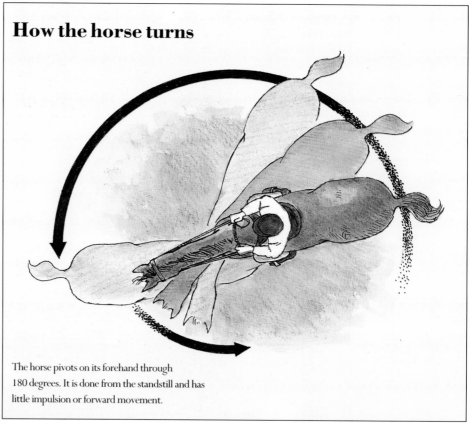

The horse pivots on its forehand through 180 degrees. It is done from the standstill and has little impulsion or forward movement.

Turn on the forehand: advanced horse

1 Starting from halt, the rider applies her left leg on the girth to ask the horse to move sideways. At the same time she restrains the horse with her hands to keep the forehand in the same place.

2 The horse's hind legs step across each other as it pivots on the forehand. The rider continues to apply the leg aid in rhythm with the movement, while her hands control the horse's shoulders.

3 The horse has turned through 180 degrees while remaining on the same spot.

Counter canter

In counter canter the horse leads with its outside foreleg, and its body is flexed slightly towards the outside of the arena. It should be just as fluid and controlled as the true canter.

The aids for counter canter are the opposite to those used for true canter. The outside leg is used on the girth and asks for strike-off, while the inside leg is used behind the girth to create impulsion and maintain the movement. The outside rein directs the horse and maintains the bend to the outside, while the inside rein helps to balance the horse and controls its speed and direction.

To begin with, practice counter canter on a shallow loop on the long side of the arena, maintaining the bend towards the direction of the leading leg. You can then move on to the two exercises illustrated here.

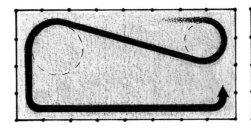

Counter cantering: circles

Ride a small circle and come back to the track in counter canter, then bring the horse back to the walk, or change back to true canter using a simple change. When the horse can do this on both reins, continue the counter canter through the corner of the arena.

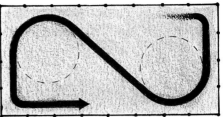

Counter cantering: figures-of-eight

When the horse can hold counter canter through the end of the school, ride a figure-of-eight, maintaining counter canter through the whole movement.

Counter canter: advanced horse

1 The rider has asked for strike-off in counter canter by using her outside leg on the girth.

2 The rider uses her inside leg slightly behind the girth to maintain the gait, and her outside leg stays on the girth.

3 Her inside hand controls the horse's direction while her outside hand helps to maintain the bend.

4 The counter-canter stride: the outside foreleg leaves the ground as the inside hind leg comes well under the horse.

Shoulder-in

In shoulder-in the horse moves forward and sideways down the track. Its forehand is a little inside the track, with its shoulders turned in, while its hindquarters remain on the track. Its body is bent around the rider's inside leg, away from the direction of travel, and its shoulders should form an angle of about 30 degrees to the track. You should aim to have the inside hind leg falling in the track left by the outside foreleg, and the horse should be flexed slightly away from the direction it is going. This will give you the correct angle to the track.

Shoulder-in is a good exercise for making the horse more supple. It is particularly good for loosening up a horse's shoulders for jumping. It also teaches the horse to listen to the rider's legs.

The best way to practice shoulder-in is to start it coming off a small circle at one end of the arena. Come around the circle imagining you are going to do another circle. As the horse's shoulders come off the track to start the second circle, resist a little with the inside rein or do a half-halt. Contain the bend with the outside hand so that the horse does not come too far around. Keeping this degree of flexion, push the horse forwards down the track with your inside leg on the girth, controlling the hindquarters with your outside leg behind the girth.

Shoulder-in is a small movement. Many people tend to think they do not have enough angle to the track, so they overdo it. Experience will teach you the angle correctly.

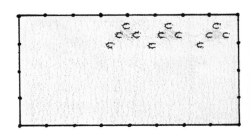

Achieving the correct angle

To achieve the correct angle to the track and to make sure that the horse moves on two tracks, the horse's outside hind leg should fall in the print left by the inside foreleg.

Correct shoulder-in: novice horse

1 The rider is using her inside leg to push the horse down the track. Her outside leg is a little behind the girth to keep the horse's hindquarters straight. Her inside hand asks for flexion in the horse's body while her outside hand controls the amount, and the horse's direction.

2 The inside hind leg is falling in the print left by the outside foreleg. This young horse is showing the movement well, and has a good angle to the track, but it needs to develop a little more flexion in the body.

Common faults

Lack of flexion

The rider is not using her legs and hands to ask the horse to flex.

Too much angle

With too much angle to the track the horse makes too many tracks with its feet. Adjust the angle by controlling the shoulders through the reins.

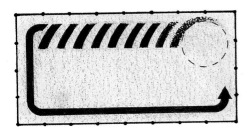

Starting the movement

Imagine that shoulder-in is a segment of a circle, and push the horse down the track keeping the same degree of flexion.

Suppleness and obedience

In order to perform the more advanced paces well, horses must spend time doing elementary exercises such as shoulder-in when they are young so that they learn to be obedient to the rider's leg.

The half-pass

In this movement the horse moves forwards and sideways down the arena on two tracks. The horse's body should remain parallel to the sides of the arena overall, although it must be flexed towards the way it is going, unlike shoulder-in, when it is flexed away from the direction in which it is going. The hindquarters must not either trail behind or get ahead of the shoulders. This exercise shows whether the horse is loose in the hips.

To practice half-pass, come around the track and ask the horse to bend in the way you are going by using the inside hand, and controlling the direction of the horse with the outside hand. Your outside leg goes behind the girth to push the horse away, while your inside leg is just on the girth to make sure that the hind quarters do not lead the movement. Look in the direction in which the horse is going.

You must aim for a good, active cross-over with the forelegs, with the hind legs stepping out as well, and you must maintain impulsion and rhythm as the horse carries out the movement.

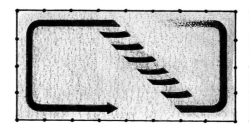

Starting the movement

As you start to come down the long side of the arena, move away from the track towards the center in half-pass.

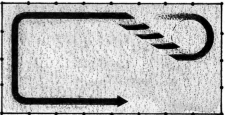

Completing the movement

Turn to come down the center of the arena and then move in half-pass either left or right back to the track. The horse should be straight as you come on to the track again.

Half-pass: novice horse

1 The rider is using her outside (left) leg behind the girth to push the horse forwards and sideways, while her inside leg controls the hindquarters.

2 The horse is performing this adequately for its stage of training, but is not yet loose enough in the shoulders to perform it well.

3 This horse needs to develop more cross-over with the forelegs, and more "expression" in the movement as a whole.

Half pass: advanced horse

The horse is using a good through action, stepping over well with its forelegs. The outside hind is also stepping out well.

Common faults

Leading with the hindquarters

The horse's hindquarters are moving across the arena fractionally ahead of the shoulders because the rider is not controlling them enough with her inside (right) leg.

Self-carriage

As a horse becomes stronger and more supple, through schooling, it develops self-carriage, or the ability to perform paces and movements with "expression", as demonstrated by this horse and by the advanced horse above.

Leg-yielding

In this movement the horse again travels forwards and sideways down the arena. It should have flexion away from the direction in which it is going. As in half-pass, aim to keep the horse parallel overall to the side of the arena. The hindquarters should neither lead nor trail behind the shoulders.

Your outside leg should stay near the girth so that it controls the horse's shoulder. If it goes too far back, it will throw the hindquarters over too much. Feel the outside rein to ask for slight flexion away from the direction the horse is going in. Your other hand controls the degree of flexion.

Leg-yielding correctly

1 The rider is using her outside (left) leg to push the horse sideways, while her inside (right) leg stays near the girth in order to prevent the horse's right shoulder from falling out.

2 At the same time the outside (left) rein is asking the horse for flexion away from the direction in which it is moving. The inside (right) rein is against the horse's neck helping to support the shoulder and controlling the amount of flexion.

Leg-yielding: loops

Ride a shallow loop down the side of the arena leg-yielding towards the center. Go straight for a few strides, then leg-yield in the other direction back to the track.

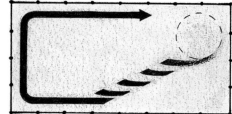

Leg-yielding: circles

Ride a small circle, and begin leg-yielding across the arena to the far track as you come off the top of it.

Walk pirouette

In walk pirouette the horse pivots on its hindquarters. You push the horse as if to move on but bring it around with the reins at the same time. It is done from the walk, and the horse should move smoothly forward into walk without hesitation as it finishes the movement. The hind legs mark time, while the forelegs step across one another. The horse must bend around your inside leg, maintaining flexion in the direction in which it is going, and must pick up its hind feet as it turns.

Prepare the horse with a half-halt and begin the movement as the inside hind stops moving forward. Push the horse on using the outside leg behind the girth, and the inside leg on the girth. At the same time use the rein to ask the horse to step around, while the outside rein controls the degree and speed of the turn.

This exercise should not be done until the horse is working in collected gaits and has good impulsion. It is good for teaching the horse to shift its weight back and lighten its forehand.

A good walk pirouette

1 The rider is using her seat and legs to push the horse on. She is showing it the way round with the inside rein, while the outside rein comes to the horse's neck to help bring it around.

2 The rider keeps applying the aids in rhythm with the horse's steps. The horse shows good flexion and is looking in the direction it is going.

3 The horse's weight is back on its hindquarters, and its forelegs are crossing over well.

4 The rider is using her leg behind the girth in case the horse's hindquarters are about to swing out.

Passage and piaffe

Passage is a very advanced dressage movement that only a few horses find easy to do. It is a very elevated form of trot that has more lift than collected trot and a definite moment of suspension. It looks like a slow-motion trot, but at the same time it must not lose energy, and the movement must be forward-going. The horse should look as if it is springing from one step to the next.

Piaffe is another very advanced movement. It is a 2-beat gait in which the horse does a very springy trot on the spot. It requires a lot of impulsion with the horse's hind legs brought well underneath it. The horse must keep itself level as it does this, and some horses find it very difficult.

Correct passage (above)

The horse is nicely up in front, everything is flexing and it is producing a very elevated stride. The rider is using a light, forward seat, and her legs are around the horse just behind the girth asking for an upward lift with each step. Her hands are distributing the energy that is created.

Correct piaffe (left)

Everything is off the floor as the horse springs from one step to another on the spot.

Riding a dressage test

Dressage tests require the horse to be active and free while still displaying all the qualities of power and speed that are its inherent characteristics. It must be light in hand so that the rider can control it with a light contact on the reins and almost invisible aids. It must be calm but keen, and forward going when asked. It must be supple and obedient, and adjust its gaits without resentment. It must remain straight from its head to its tail when moving on a straight line, bending slightly in the direction it is traveling on a curved line. All gaits must maintain a regular rhythm with the correct footfall.

In addition, all changes of gait and other movements must take place at the specified markers, your circles must be circles, serpentines must be evenly spaced, and circles and loops must be the specified size.

Competitions are judged by one to three judges, and by five at international level. Each judge has a writer to note down the points scored and comments for each movement. Each movement is marked out of 10 points. In addition, extra points are given for different aspects of your overall performance: for example, general impression and calmness; accuracy of gaits and impulsion; and the position and seat of the rider and correct application of the aids.

You should aim to arrive early at a competition to give yourself and your horse plenty of time to relax and unwind after the journey. This is not the time for a final practice. Do a few simple movements to warm up and get the horse listening to you.

After the test study the judges' remarks on your score sheet carefully, and work extra hard at the movements you have been marked down on before next time.

Interpreting your dressage marks

In competition, whatever your level, you will be marked on a scale of 0–10. The judges award marks based on the expected performance for the class you have entered.

0	Not Performed.
1	Very bad.
2	Bad.
3	Fairly Bad.
4	Insufficient
5	Sufficient
6	Satisfactory
7	Fairly Good.
8	Good.
9	Very Good.
10	Excellent.

Preparing to compete

Horse and rider have a final brush-up and warm-up before going in for their test.

EVENTING

Eventing requires horse and rider to be proficient in all three disciplines – dressage, cross-country and show-jumping. However, the cross-country phase is the key to success, and in this section we look at the training and the jumping techniques required by this demanding sport.

In planning a cross-country course, the course-builder takes full advantage of the natural terrain in planning obstacles to test the ability and courage of horse and rider.

The basic principles of good communication apply more than ever when you are riding over a tough course, as you have to guide and encourage your horse through daunting obstacles and over difficult terrain.

Athletic jumping

A good, athletic jump out of the water.

Table fence (left)

Eventing requires strong jumping over large fences.

Mark Phillips (above)

Mark Phillips competing at Badminton Horse Trials, 1982.

Good communication (right)

Good communication between horse and rider is vital if they are to get round a course successfully.

Safety equipment

If you are going to take up eventing, you should fit out yourself and your horse with the necessary safety equipment, even before you start jumping practice courses. It is a risky sport and you should take every possible step to avoid injury to yourself and your horse.

At novice level, your usual saddle and bridle will be adequate, but it is a good idea to replace the reins with rubber-covered, non-slip ones. Your horse should be wearing protective boots.

Before a competition, check all the tack for signs of wear and tear, and make sure that the stitching is still firm. Have any repairs done immediately, and replace any item that looks as if it is no longer secure.

It is unwise to change your horse's tack just before a competition, as it will not have time to get used to the new tack. If you are worried that your horse might become very headstrong when it goes around a cross-country course, ask your instructor or a knowledgeable friend for advice on what bit to use to give you more control.

For the rider, an approved, well-fitting crash hat is compulsory for eventing. In competition, you should also wear a body-protector to guard your spine and ribs should you fall.

The horse's tack (above)

The horse is wearing a regular saddle and snaffle bridle, surcingle, breast-plate with running martingale attachment, which prevents the saddle from slipping back as the horse jumps, and protective boots.

Surcingle (below)

A surcingle, or over-girth, is a wide strap that passes round the horse's body over the top of the saddle and girth. It provides some protection to the rider should the girth suddenly break.

Protective boots

The horse is wearing fetlock boots to protect its front legs should it hit a fence (right). Overreach boots (far right) protect the horse's heels if it should strike them with its back feet either as it jumps or as it gallops over uneven ground.

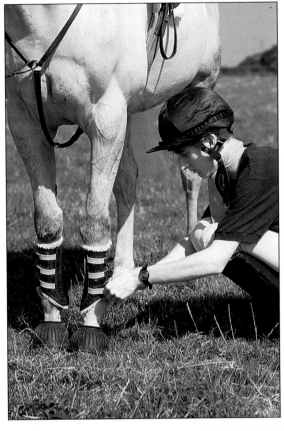

Racing breastplate (far left)

This type of breastplate consists of a wide strap around the front of the horse's chest attached to a neckstrap and to either side of the front of the saddle.

The rider (left)

It is a good precaution to wear a body-protector under your jersey. There are several different types available, and you should look around for one which is comfortable.

The cross-country position

A cross-country course is ridden at speed. As the horse gallops around, it stretches out and its center of gravity moves forward. The key to riding a course well is to adopt a forward seat in order to stay in balance with the horse.

You should fold forward from the hip, with your seat out of the saddle, and keep your lower leg securely in position all the time. As you come in to a fence sit lightly in the saddle in order to drive the horse on over it.

It is vital that your legs remain in the correct position, firmly on the girth, all the time if you are to remain secure in the saddle. If they slide out of position, or flap against the horse's side, you will not be able to maintain a secure position.

Work all the time to remain in balance with the horse, not getting either ahead of or behind its movement.

The correct position (above)

The rider's weight is forward, and she is well balanced over the horse. Her lower leg is vertical, and is steady against the horse's side. She is pushing her weight down into her heel. She is maintaining a straight line from her elbow through her hands to the horse's mouth, keeping up a firm contact and good communication.

A secure position (left)

A good, secure position in the saddle will enable you to tackle any type of obstacle with confidence.

Second nature

Awkward fences such as this drop into water show how important it is that a good position in the saddle becomes second nature to the rider. Here, the rider is leaning back to keep his weight over the horse's center of gravity as they tackle the big drop, but he is still keeping his leg firmly in position on the girth.

Common faults

Poor rider position

The rider's leg is too far back, and she is leaning forwards to compensate. This brings her ahead of the horse's movement, shifting her weight too far forward and making it difficult for her to apply her lower leg properly. She has lowered her hands, so the line of contact from her elbow to the horse's mouth has been broken.

Gridwork

Gridwork is as valuable in training the event horse as it is in the other areas of competition. It builds the horse's confidence by teaching it to think for itself, and to shorten and lengthen its stride coming to a fence. It is particularly good for practicing combinations as it teaches the horse to maintain its concentration over a series of fences.

Grids can be used to practice different types of fences and to solve specific problems as you can vary the jumps and the distances between them. You can bring two fences close together to create a bounce fence. Or you can space the fences apart with poles on the ground between them to make an over-eager horse concentrate.

Start with one pole and a single fence and build up gradually from there, but do not confront your horse with a mass of poles. It saves a lot of time if you can have a helper at

A straightforward grid

1 The grid starts with crosspoles, which guide the horse in to the center of the grid, and encourage it to round over the fence.

hand to move fences and put back fallen poles for you.

It is very important that you get the distances in the grid right for your horse. All horses are different, so you need to work out the length of your horse's stride in relation to your own paces, in order to assess distances accurately.

Setting up a practice grid (below)

Practice on this type of grid helps you and the horse to judge the length of stride. The distance between the elements depends on whether you are in trot or canter.

2 The pole on the ground brings the horse to the second fence correctly. It is looking confident and alert as it takes off.

Approximate distances for setting up a grid		
Approach	**In trot**	**In canter**
Bounce	9-11ft	11-14ft
	2.75–3.3m	3.3-4.25m
One non-jumping stride	18–24ft	24–26ft
	5.5–7.3m	7.3–7.9m
Two non-jumping strides	30–32ft	34–36ft
	9–9.75m	10.4–11m

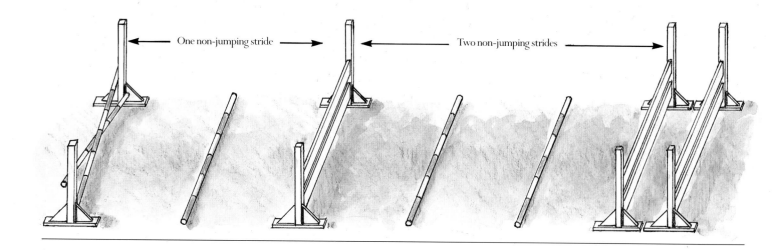

One non-jumping stride   Two non-jumping strides

3 The canter poles between the fences teach an over-enthusiastic horse to bring its head down and concentrate, and discourage it from rushing at the next fence.

4 The horse jumps well over the last element. The rider is in balance, with her weight forward, lower legs on the girth, and hands maintaining good contact with the horse's mouth.

Common faults

Pacing out the distances

You need to know the length of your horse's stride in relation to your own. You can then set up a grid to suit your own horse by pacing out the distance between each element.

Rushing the fence

1 As the horse rushes at the last fence in the grid, it takes its rider by surprise. She is almost sitting back in the saddle, having been left behind the horse's movement.

2 Because the horse rushed at the fence, it has flattened out over it, raising its head and hollowing its back, and risking knocking it down. The rider is still behind the movement.

Gridwork: improving an impetuous horse

If you have an over-eager horse that tends to rush the fences, you can work on the problem by constantly changing the grid, and making it more demanding. If the horse is constantly being presented with something new, it will have to keep thinking and concentrating.

As with all gridwork, it is important that you frequently change the rein to keep the horse balanced and supple. This can be done by jumping a grid in reverse.

Gridwork will teach this type of horse to concentrate, to go more calmly and to think about what it is doing.

Jumping the grid

1 The horse rounds over the fence well. It is alert and concentrating. The rider is a little ahead of the horse's movement, possibly in anticipation of the horse rushing the fence.

2 The horse lifts itself well up over the second element in the grid. The rider has slightly raised her hands, reducing the effectiveness of her contact with the horse's mouth.

3 The rider is well balanced over the horse, and is driving it on with her legs, persuading it to maintain its concentration over the final element.

Neat jumping (left)

David Wilding Davies and Crusader in action at Badminton Horse Trials, 1989.

2

Corner fences (below)

Corner fences require positive, powerful jumping.

3

Common faults

Restrictive hands

The rider's hands have too tight a contact on the horse's mouth, restricting its movement. As a result, the horse raises its head and hollows its outline as it lands.

Gridwork: improving a sluggish horse

This type of horse lacks natural impulsion, and needs constant driving with the leg to make up for it. Gridwork will make it more supple and athletic, and will teach it to stretch out and lengthen its stride. However, do not do too much work over grids or it may start to back off.

You can improve this type of horse by schooling over single fences as well. Really ride it hard and encourage it to go at the fence. It will also benefit from being schooled in a group to bring out its competitive spirit.

This type of horse will need plenty of encouragement as well as very firm riding as it takes the grid.

Lack of impulsion

1 The lack of impulsion in the horse results in a laborious jump. The rider has moved too far forward in an attempt to "lift" the horse up over the fence. In so doing, her legs have moved back and her hands have lifted, breaking her lines of communication with the horse.

2 The canter poles on the ground encourage the horse to lengthen its stride between the elements. However, the rider's hands are still too high, so she cannot contain the horse's movement.

3 As a result, the horse comes in too close to the crosspoles. The rider still does not have proper contact with the horse's mouth, and she has got too far forward again. She is giving the horse confusing instructions and it could easily have stopped.

4 Although the horse takes off very close to the crosspoles it is making a good shape over the fence.

Going well

1 The rider is sitting down in the saddle and is really pushing the horse on by closing her lower legs hard against it in rhythm with its strides. The horse responds by coming in with plenty of impulsion.

2 The horse springs out and rounds well over the first fence.

3 The two poles on the ground have been replaced by a single one to make the horse really stretch. The rider is using her legs hard again to ask the horse to lengthen its stride, and is maintaining a firm contact with the horse's mouth.

4 The horse does not get in too close this time, and it springs off with plenty of energy.

Cross-country fences

Cross-country requires more than the ability to jump well. Confidence and courage are needed in horse and rider in order to tackle the wide range of obstacles that are thrown at them. Indecision or fear on your part will communicate themselves to your horse, causing refusals, falls and half-hearted attempts at jumps.

Jumps are sited in awkward positions, at the top and bottom of steep hills, going uphill or downhill, angled across a slope, or going from sunlight into deep shadow, or an open space into a gloomy group of trees, and vice versa.

It is also not just a matter of jumping uprights and spreads; the jumps come in many different disguises. Combinations become bounce fences, and may be sited going uphill or downhill. Corner fences, table fences, steps, jumps into and out of water, also sometimes on the uphill or downhill, are just some of the obstacles you will have to tackle. With a little help you can build some of these types of fences at home to practice over.

Variation on a zig-zag (above)

This type of fence should be treated like a spread. It should be approached with plenty of impulsion, and the horse should be brought in close to the base of the fence for take-off.

Corner fence (left)

The corner fence is one of the most difficult on a cross-country course. The rider is encouraging his horse on as it struggles to clear the corner.

Drop fence (left)

Ruth Williams and Conspirator look calm and confident as they land over a straightforward drop fence. She is remaining slightly upright in the saddle in order to keep her weight in balance with the horse.

Water fence (right)

Bruce Davidson on JJ Babu takes a spectacular combination of water and uphill steps. Cross-country obstacles sometimes consist of daunting combinations of different types of fences.

Bounce fences

On a cross-country course you are quite likely to meet a 'bounce' fence. This is a form of combination fence where there is no non-jumping stride between the elements. The horse lands over the first part and immediately takes off for the second.

You can practice riding a bounce either on its own or as part of your grid. As your horse grows in confidence and experience, you could even try a double bounce.

This type of fence places great demands on a horse's athleticism and co-ordination. As its forelegs touch the ground over the first element, it must bring its hindquarters as far underneath it as possible to take off for the second part.

To tackle a bounce fence successfully the horse needs to be supple and agile. You need to bring it in on a short, controlled stride, well balanced and with plenty of impulsion. If the horse comes in long and flat, it will probably land too far over the first element and have trouble with the second. You should sit up slightly between the elements so that you do not push the horse on to its forehand as it lifts itself up over the second element.

With this type of fence in particular, it is very important that your position follows through with the jump of the horse so that you do not get ahead of or behind it. You must keep your weight pushing down into your heels and let your hands go forward with the horse's movement, keeping in communication with the horse all the way.

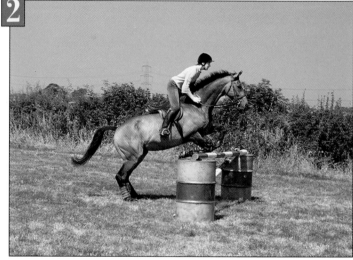

Taking a bounce fence

1 The rider is sitting down and using her seat, legs and hands to bring the horse in on a short, bouncy, controlled, well-balanced stride. Its hocks are well underneath it and it has plenty of impulsion.

2 The horse lifts itself up well over the fence, although the rider's position is a little forward of the movement.

3 As the horse lands over the first part, it brings its hocks well underneath it in preparation to spring off over the second part. The rider sits up slightly, applies her lower leg and allows the horse's movement with her hands.

Common faults

Poor contact with the reins

1 Rather than going forwards with the horse's movement, the rider has dropped her hands, so that they pull down on the horse's mouth and prevent it stretching its head and neck forward sufficiently.

2 As a result, the horse has flattened out over the fence, raising its head and hollowing its outline. Its hindquarters are trailing over the fence and risk knocking it down.

Downhill bounce

1 Horse and rider take off over the first part of a downhill bounce fence. A straight approach and neat, athletic jumping are essential for this type of fence.

2 The rider has her weight back as they land over the first part. The partnership looks confident and well balanced.

3 The horse has brought its hocks under and taken off close to the second part. They look set to clear it comfortably.

Corner fences

Corner fences can be awkward obstacles when you first meet them in competition. Approached correctly, however, they shouldn't cause too many problems.

Try setting up a practice jump, using a couple of poles and three jump stands. Start with the jump quite low and the angle between the poles quite narrow. As your schooling progresses and you and your horse become more confident, you can open out the angle and increase the height of the jump as necessary.

This type of fence can easily confuse your horse if you are not clear in your approach to it. Cut across the corner and you run the risk of the horse running out (remember that in a competition there won't be a jump stand – possibly just a flag). Approach the jump riding across but away from the corner and you still present the horse with problems. It will have to tackle the widest part of the spread, and the front pole will be angling outward toward it making take-off difficult.

The best way to tackle this type of fence is straight on but toward the corner so that the spread is not too great. It is particularly important that you keep the horse going straight and forward for this type of fence, which has a wide spread and can be quite demanding. If the jump becomes an effort, the horse will start to lose confidence.

Jumping a corner fence

1 Horse and rider approach toward the center of the fence. The rider is sitting well down in the saddle. She is really working at pushing the horse on and sticking to her line of approach, and the horse is quite clear about what is being asked of it.

2 At the point of take-off the horse's weight is well balanced over its hocks. The rider keeps her weight pushing down into her heels as she starts to fold forward.

The correct angle

Approach a corner fence straight on but near the corner.

Common faults

Backing off

The approach to the fence is on the side away from the corner, and the horse is backing off. The rider needs to push the horse forward more in order to encourage it to lengthen its stride into the fence.

Indecisive approach

1 The horse is heading towards the corner instead of meeting the fence straight on and is approaching in a hesitant manner. The rider is not using her whip enough, nor is she sitting down in the saddle. She needs to use her outside leg much more to keep the horse straight, and to maintain firmer contact with the outside rein.

2 Lack of confidence in the approach is communicated with the result that it runs out.

3 As they go over the jump, the rider's position is good. Her hands are forward but haven't dropped, and she has folded forward from the hip, making it easier for the horse to stretch out over the spread and tuck up its front legs.

4 Horse and rider land well in balance, ready to ride on to the next fence.

Table fences

These big solid fences are always found on a cross-country round. Although they appear solid and imposing, they are easier to jump than they look. If you approach them with plenty of impulsion and plenty of control they should ride well.

A table fence should be treated like a spread. That is, you should come in on a lengthening stride and get close in for take-off. However, although they have a very solid top line, they usually do not have a proper ground line, and it is easy to come in too close. You need to judge the take-off point very carefully.

With any type of fence you need to bear in mind that you should always adjust the way you ride to the temperament and ability of the horse you are on. If you do this, you will be able to help the horse to jump to the best of its ability. If you have an impetuous, over-eager horse, sit up a little to control it as you approach a fence and let the fence come to you. If you are on a more sluggish horse, sit down in the saddle and drive the horse on hard with the legs, in rhythm wiht the horse's strides, in order to create the necessary speed and impulsion. Fold right down over the fence so that the horse can really stretch out over it.

Log piles

A solid, square pile of logs needs to be ridden accurately and with plenty of impulsion.

Impetuous horse

1 This horse needs little encouragement to jump. The rider is asking the horse to take the jump steadily by remaining slightly upright in the saddle in order to hold the horse's natural exuberance in check.

2 The horse springs out well over the fence. The rider's leg position remains secure and he is folding forward from the hip.

Sluggish horse

1 This horse lacks natural impulsion, and has to be encouraged over the fence. The rider drives the horse on hard with her legs as they approach take-off.

2 As they go over the fence she folds down as much as possible to allow the horse to stretch to its maximum to make up for any lack of impulsion on take-off.

Lucinda Green (right)

Lucinda Green on Shannagh at Badminton, 1986. Table fences of all sorts require strong, accurate riding, but are quite straightforward.

Drop fences

A drop fence, that is, a fence where the ground is lower on the landing side than on the take-off side, can strike terror in the heart of even experienced cross-country riders.

The secret is to come in very steadily – preferably at the trot – making sure that the horse is balanced and that its weight is well back on its hindquarters. The horse must not be in danger of falling onto its forehand. Bring the horse in as close as possible to the fence, with its hocks well underneath it. Keep fairly upright to help the horse lift itself up, and aim for a neat jump over the top. If you take the jump slowly you reduce the risk of the horse jarring itself on landing.

If the horse stands off at a drop fence, it will land a long way out from the fence, where the ground will fall away more steeply. The horse may jarr itself as it lands, and an inexperienced rider whose balance and position are not quite secure will be thrown forwards.

You can easily be thrown out of position over this type of jump if you do not go with the horse's movement all the way. Keep your leg position secure and do not interfere as the horse stretches over the fence. Allow with your hands, letting the reins slip through your fingers so that the horse can stretch its head and neck as far downwards as it needs to, to balance itself on landing.

Taking a drop fence

1 This is a cautious horse, and it is coming in steadily. The rider is sitting down in the saddle, and is squeezing with her legs to create an active pace while keeping good contact through her hands with the horse's mouth.

3 Because the horse took off close to the fence it lands reasonably close in, and is not jarred by the landing. The rider is allowing the horse to stretch its head and neck right out in order to balance itself, but at the same time is maintaining good contact with the horse's mouth.

2 By pushing on with her legs the rider has made the horse bring its hocks well underneath it, close in to the fence, for take-off. The rider has her weight well balanced above the horse as it rounds over the fence.

Lack of control

1 The horse is approaching at a trot, but it is "running" at the fence because the rider is not controlling the pace. The rider is too far back in the saddle and is pulling back on the reins. He needs to use his legs to make the horse bring its hocks underneath it, and to contain the horse's movement with his hands, in order to create a more active pace.

2 The rider is pulling on the reins in an attempt to contain the horse's movement. The horse is trying to stretch out against the pull of the rider's hand, and is having difficulty lifting its forehand up over the fence.

3 The rider has fallen behind the horse's movement, with his weight right back in the saddle. However, he is allowing with the reins as much as he can from this position.

4 Horse and rider have remained in balance, but have landed a long way out from the fence, where the ground is falling away.

Downhill fences

Downhill fences require a similar style of riding to drop fences. However, the approach may be downhill for a while before you reach the jump, and it can be difficult to maintain a good, balanced approach. You should come in on a controlled stride, and always take a downhill fence straight.

It is very important to follow the natural movement of the horse, keeping a more upright position in the saddle so that your weight does not move forward ahead of the point of balance for the horse. Allow with the hands so that the horse can stretch its head and neck down without restriction to keep its balance on landing. You must remain balanced and independent of your hands (see page 66) throughout the jump.

Make sure that you get in close to this type of fence. If the horse stands off, it cannot see where it will land and may be reluctant to take the jump.

Jumping downhill

The rider has his weight right back and is giving the horse its head so that it can balance itself on landing.

Taking a downhill fence

1 Horse and rider have made a balanced approach. The rider is driving with his legs as they come into the fence, and the horse has brought its hocks well underneath it. They arrive close in for take-off.

2 The rider has stayed slightly upright as they go over the fence and his leg remains in a secure position, keeping him balanced, and allowing him to follow the natural movement of the horse. His hands have a good contact with the horse's mouth.

3 On landing the rider lets the reins slip through his fingers, so that the horse has complete freedom to balance itself. His legs have remained in position, and he is completely balanced and secure in the saddle.

A steep slope

The rider has his weight well back as the horse lands on this steeply sloping obstacle.

Uphill fences

Uphill fences require a lot of impulsion in the horse to give it the necessary thrust to bring its hocks underneath it and spring up and over the fence.

You and your horse must be well balanced coming up the hill on the approach, and you must be coming in with a very bouncy stride. You create this by squeezing hard with the legs and controlling the horse's forward movement with your hands.

The key to jumping this type of fence is to keep with the horse all the way up the hill, and to keep your weight forward over the horse as it jumps the fence so that you do not interfere with its natural action.

You can easily get left behind on take-off, which will throw your weight back over the horse's hindquarters and make it difficult for the horse to spring up off its hocks. If you are leaning back, you are also in danger of restricting the movement of the horse's head and neck.

Standing off (above)

Standing off at an uphill fence will make it seem much larger than it is.

Positive riding (left)

Uphill fences require bold uphill riding and tremendous impulsion.

Taking an uphill fence

1 Although the rider has got a little behind the horse's movement as it took off, he is aware of the problem and has extended his arms right forward in order not to restrict the horse.

2 The rider is still too far back in the saddle but his legs are securely on the horse, and he is well balanced over it. He is not restricting the horse, which is stretching out well over the fence.

3 The rider has remained secure in the saddle, which has enabled him to recover to a good position quickly on landing.

Common faults

Lack of balance

The horse is having to twist itself up over the fence because it has come in on an unbalanced stride.

Steps: downhill

Many riders are worried by steps when they first come across them. However, they are really a series of downhill or uphill fences in quick succession, and should be approached in the same way.

Downhill Steps

Approach downhill steps on a controlled, well-balanced stride. Take them steadily and do not try to do a big jump. Between each step come upright, and put the leg on firmly to tell the horse that you want it to keep going. Keep your hands flexible, following the horse's movement as it stretches over each part.

Taking downhill steps

1 The rider's contact is good but he is not pushing the horse on quite strongly enough with the legs, so the horse falters at the top of the first step.

2 The horse's hesitation was momentary. The rider is secure and well balanced in the saddle, staying with the action of the horse. He has come more upright in the saddle and is using the leg firmly to encourage the horse to keep going down the second step.

Steps down

Landing over the first of four steps down horse and rider look well balanced and secure.

3 As the horse takes off, the rider has come forward of the movement.

4 The rider has recovered his position in the saddle and lands in balance and with the movement. If you are ahead of the movement, there is always the danger that you will be pitched forwards on landing.

Steps: uphill

Steps uphill are jumped in the same way as for other uphill fences. You need to have tremendous impulsion, and to drive the horse on with a strong leg so that you do not lose momentum half-way up. Keep your lower leg firmly on the girth and your weight well forward. Once you begin to get behind the movement, you will fall further behind with each jump up.

Steps up (above)

Angela Tucker on Charleston V demonstrates the impulsion and forward riding necessary for taking uphill steps.

Taking uphill steps

1 As they approach the bottom step, the rider is sitting down in the saddle and is pushing hard with the seat and legs to create plenty of impulsion.

2 As they land over the first step, the rider has got behind the movement with his weight a long way back in the saddle. This is restricting the horse's forward movement.

Steps up (above)

Horse and rider demonstrate good balance and tremendous impulsion as they attack these steps with confidence.

3 The horse takes off strongly up the second step, but the rider's weight is hanging back and his lower leg is starting to creep forwards.

4 As they land over the second step, the rider's weight has fallen even further back in the saddle than over the first. However, he is stretching forward with his hands in order to restrict the horse's movement as much as possible.

Water fences

Water fences are a common feature of cross-country courses, and the sooner you and your horse get used to jumping in and out of water the better.

Introduce your horse to water gradually. Take it to a nearby stream, having first checked that the stream-bed is fairly even and stable, and let it have a good look at the water before you encourage it to go in. Spend some time paddling around and walking through it so that the horse feels completely at ease. If you have a second horse with you who is used to water, it can take the lead and encourage the inexperienced one to go in.

Water creates drag as you move through it, slowing the horse up quite suddenly, and you need to be prepared for this as you jump into it.

If you come in fast and flat to water fences, you will probably be tipped forwards as the horse lands and the water checks its forward movement. On the other hand, if you are not pushing the horse on enough, it may well stop. Approach them at a steady pace and with plenty of impulsion.

Once you have jumped into the water, sit up and control the horse, bringing it back to trot if you can. This will give the spray a chance to settle so that the horse can see the jump out.

Well balanced approach (above)

Horse and rider are well balanced as they drop down into the water.

1988 Olympics (left)

Bruce Davidson and Dr Peaches land neatly in the water at the Seoul Olympics.

Helping the horse (left)

The rider gives the horse its head as it lands in the water.

Spray (left)

Spray can cause a problem when you are jumping in water. If you can, bring your horse back to a trot so that the spray has a chance to settle.

A typical water jump (above)

Claus Erhorn on Justyn Thyme taking the water jump at Burghley, 1989.

Glossary

Aids Recognized signals used by a rider to pass instructions to his mount. *Artificial aids* include whips, spurs and ancillary items of tack used by a rider to assist him in giving aids. *Natural aids* are the rider's hands, legs, body or voice. *Diagonal aids* are aids in which opposite hands and legs are used simultaneously, i.e., the right rein is used with the left leg. *Lateral aids* are hand and leg aids given together on the same side.

Balanced The horse carries its own weight and that of its rider evenly.

Bars (of mouth) Fleshy area between the front and back teeth on either side of a horse's mouth.

Bay A deep, rich, reddish-brown colored horse, with black mane, tail, and lower legs.

Bit Mouthpiece often made of metal, rubber or vulcanite placed in the horse's mouth and kept in position by the bridle to aid the rider's control. *Curb bits* include any one of a number of bits, the mouthpieces of which vary in design but which include hooks on either side to which a curb chain or strap is attached. This lies in the horse's chin groove and gives the bit its characteristic leverage action. A *gag bit* is a particularly severe form of bit. It may be raised to a greater or lesser degree, thus affecting the severity of the bit. A *snaffle bit* is any one of a number of designs of bit that act on the corners or bars of the mouth. The bit takes only one pair of reins.

Bitless bridle Bridle without bit. Control is achieved by concentrating pressure on the nose and chin groove. A *bosal* is a very simple bitless bridle, the term actually referring to the rawhide noseband which is its chief component. A *hackamore* is the most widely known type of bitless bridle.

Boarding (stables) Riding establishment where an owner may keep his horse for a fee.

Box, to To lead a horse into a horse van or trailer.

Break in, to Training the young horse to accept and respond to a rider on his back.

Broken wind Permanent disability to a horse's respiratory system manifesting in a chronic, persistent and rasping cough.

Brushing Striking of the inside hind or foreleg with its opposite. May lead to injury and lameness.

Cavalletti Adjustable low wooden jump used in the schooling of horse or rider in jumping.

Cavesson Either a simple noseband fitted to a bridle, or a more sophisticated piece of equipment worn by a horse when he is to be lunged (q.v.). In the latter, it is sometimes referred to as a *breaking cavesson*.

Chestnut An overall yellowish-brown coat, with the mane and tail possibly the same color.

Cob A type of horse characterized by its smallness and strong, stocky build.

Collection To pull a schooled horse together by creating impulsion (q.v.) with the legs and containing it with the hands. As a result, the horse brings its hind legs more under its body, and shortens its outline (q.v.).

Colt A male, ungelded horse up to four years old.

Combination fence A series of two (a double q.v.) or three (a treble q.v.) fences placed to allow one or two strides between each fence.

Concussion Jarring of a horse's legs, usually caused by fast trotting on the road, or considerable hard work on hard ground. May result in swelling and lameness.

Counter canter School movement in which the horse canters in a circle with the outside leg leading instead of the inside leg as usual.

Curb chain Single or double link chain attached to the hooks of a curb bit and lying flat in a horse's chin groove.

Diagonals (left, right) A rider rides on the left or right diagonal at the trot depending on whether he rises as the horse's left or right foreleg moves forward. On a circle, the rider should always rise as the outside foreleg moves forward.

Disunited (canter) Canter in which the horse's legs are out of sequence. Also called cross-cantering.

Double Two fences with only a short distance between them which the horse has to jump as a combination.

Double bridle A traditional bridle with two bits, a snaffle and a curb, each with its own cheek-pieces and rein. The double bridle is more sophisticated than the snaffle, which merely raises the horse's head. The curb causes the horse to flex its neck and bring its nose in, giving the rider greater control than a bridle with one bit.

Draw rein Severe form of control comprised of a rein attached at one end to the girth, which passes through the bit rings and back to the rider's hands.

Dressage The art of training a horse so that he is totally obedient and responsible to his rider, as well as agile and fluent in his performance.

Drop fence An obstacle in which the landing side is considerably lower than the take-off side.

Drop noseband Noseband which buckles beneath the bit to prevent the horse from opening its mouth to 'take hold' of the bit, making it easier to ignore the rider's commands.

Dun Generally refers to a 'yellow' coat with black mane, tail, legs and dorsal stripe. Also called buckskin.

Eventing Riding in a one or three day event, which combines dressage, cross-country and show jumping.

Extension The lengthening of a horse's stride at any gait. It does not necessarily mean an increase in speed.

Farrier A skilled craftsman who shoes horses.

Fetlock (joint) The lowest joint on a horse's legs.

Filly A female horse up to the age of four years old.

Flash noseband A combination of a cavesson and a drop noseband. It keeps the bit very stable in the horse's mouth.

Flexion A slight bend in the neck or body of the horse in a required direction.

Flying change When in canter, at the rider's request the horse changes the leading leg (front and back) in the moment of suspension.

Foal A horse of either sex up to the age of one year old. Male foals are usually referred to as colt foals, females as filly foals.

Fodder Any type of food stuff fed to horses.

Forehand Front part of the horse including the head, neck, shoulders, and forelegs.

Frog V-shaped leathery part found on the soles of a horse's feet which acts as a shock absorber and as an anti-slip device.

Gait The paces at which a horse moves. Usually, a walk, trot, canter or gallop.

Galls Sores caused by ill-fitting saddlery.

Gamgee Gauze-covered cotton wool used beneath stable or exercise leg bandages for extra warmth or protection.

Gelding A castrated male horse.

Grackle noseband Thin-strapped noseband with double straps buckling above and below the bit.

Gray Refers to any color horse from pure white to dark gray. Further described by such terms as 'dappled' (small iron-gray circles on a lighter background), 'flea-bitten' (specks of gray on a white background), etc.

Groom Person who looks after the daily welfare of a horse.

Grooming kit The various brushes and other tools used in cleaning a horse's coat.

Ground line Pole or similar placed in front of a fence to help horse and rider judge the take-off point.

Hack A type of horse characterized by its pleasing appearance, fine bone structure, good manners and complete obedience to its rider's commands. Also a term used to describe going for a ride.

Half pass Dressage movement performed on two tracks in which the horse moves forwards and sideways simultaneously.

Half volte A school movement in which a horse is asked to leave the track and perform a half-circle of a given diameter after which he rejoins the track to continue in the opposite direction.

Hand The recognized measurement used for determining the height of a horse or pony. A hand equals 10cm (4 ins).

Haynet Large net or bag made of rope designed to hold a horse's hay.

High school The classical art of riding, in which the traditional advanced school or dressage figures are practiced.

Hock The joint in the center part of a horse's hindlegs. Responsible for most of the horse's forward force.

Hoof pick A small metal implement with a pointed hook on one end used to remove dirt, stones, etc. from a horse's hooves.

Horn The hard, insensitive, outer covering of the hoof.

Horse van Self-propelled vehicle used for the transportation of horses.

Horsemanship The art of equitation or horse riding.

Horsemastership The art of caring for and attending to all aspects of a horse's welfare, under all possible circumstances.

Hunter Any type of horse considered suitable to be ridden to hounds.

Impulsion Strong but controlled forward movement in a horse. The rider creates impulsion with seat and legs, and controls the movement with the hands.

Indirect rein The opposite rein to the direction in which a horse is turning. When giving an indirect rein aid, the instruction to turn comes by pressing the opposite rein against the horse's neck. See also Neck reining.

Inside leg The leg or legs of rider or horse on the inside of any circle or track being described.

Irons Stirrup irons are metal items of tack attached to the saddle by the stirrup leathers to hold the feet.

Jumping lane A narrow track, usually fenced on either side in which a series of jumps are placed.

Keeper Small leather loops found on the straps of a bridle, designed to contain the end of the strap after it has been buckled, giving a neat appearance.

Lateral work School movements in which the hindlegs follow a separate track from the forelegs.

Leading leg The front leg at a canter or gallop that appears to be leading the leg sequence.

Long reins Long webbing reins attached to the bit of a horse's bridle and used in the animal's training.

Lunge, to The act of training a horse by directing it around in a circle while on a long 'lunge' rein. This rein is attached to a cavesson (q.v.). Schooled horses may be lunged as a form of exercise or during the course of teaching a novice rider.

Lunge rein A long, webbed rein used in the above action.

Manège A marked out area or school used for the teaching, training, and schooling of horse and rider.

Mare A female horse over four years old.

Martingale A device designed to prevent a horse raising its head far enough to evade the bit. A standing martingale, which has a neck strap, goes from the noseband to the girth and is attached to both. A running martingale, which also has a neck strap, goes from the girth to a small ring around each rein – in the case of a double bridle, to the snaffle rein. The Irish martingale is simply two rings at either end of a short strip of leather which has the reins passed through it at the front of the horse's neck.

Mucking out Daily stable chore involving the removal of dirty, soiled bedding and sweeping of the stable floor before replacing the bed.

Nearside The left hand side of a horse.

Neck reining The art of turning a horse by using the indirect (q.v.) or opposite rein to the direction of the turn.

Neckstrap A simple leather strap buckled around the horse's neck used to give added security to a novice rider. Also refers to the strap of a martingale that buckles around the horse's neck.

Numnah A pad worn under the saddle, usually cut in the shape of the saddle. It may be made of felt, rubber or sheepskin.

Offside The right hand side of a horse.

Outline The shape of the top line of the horse from

the head and neck, along the back, round the hindquarters to the hocks. The outline should be rounded, with the hocks underneath the horse.

Overbend A horse that has arched its neck acutely, thereby bringing its head too far into its chest. Usually caused by a rider exerting too much pressure on the reins while urging the horse forward. Also called overflexed.

Overtracking The hind feet fall slightly ahead of the prints left by the forefeet.

Paddock Fenced-in area of grassland in which horses are turned out. Generally used to denote a fairly small area.

Palomino Color of horse. The coat may be various shades of gold and the mane and tail white.

Pelham Various types of curb bit with a single mouthpiece. One or two reins can be attached. It aims to combine the snaffle and curb bits of a double bridle in a single mouthpiece.

Piebald Refers to a coat irregularly marked with large patches of black and white. Pinto is an American term for piebald and skewbald horses (q.v.).

Pirouette A dressage movement in which the forelegs describe a small circle while the hindlegs remain in the same spot, one of them acting as a pivot.

Points (of a horse) Names given to the different parts of a horse. Also used to describe the mane, tail and lower legs.

Pommel The center front of an astride saddle. In some designs, the pommel is more pronounced.

Pony A small horse that stands 14.2 hands high or less.

Port A raised section in the center mouthpiece of some curb bits. It may be raised to a greater or lesser degree, thus affecting the severity of the bit.

Pull, to (mane and tail) The process of thinning the mane and tail.

Rein back To instruct the horse to move backwards. In order to execute the movement correctly, the horse must move back with the diagonal fore-and hindlegs moving in unison.

Renvers A school movement also known as quarters-out, in which the horse moves along the side of the school, his hindlegs on the track and his forelegs on an inside track.

Rising trot The action of a rider rising from the saddle in rhythm with a horse's trot. Also called posting.

Roan Color of horse. A blue roan refers to a coat in which black and white hairs are mixed giving an overall blue effect; a strawberry roan refers to a coat in which chestnut and white hairs are mixed to give an overall reddish effect.

Roller A strap which passes around the horse's back and belly used to keep blankets in place.

Saddle horse A horse suitable for riding, as opposed to one that works in harness.

Saddle soap Specially prepared soap to be rubbed into the leather of all saddlery to help preserve it.

Saddlery A comprehensive term for all equipment worn by a horse.

School Marked-out area used for training and exercising horses and riders. To school is the art of obedience training and education of the horse.

Self-carriage The natural, good carriage of the horse without interference from the rider. The dressage horse should develop self-carriage in all gaits and movements.

Serpentine A school movement in which the horse, at any gait, moves down the center of the school in a series of equal-sized loops.

Shoe, to The act of fitting and securing metal shoes to the horse's feet, usually done by a farrier (q.v.).

Shoulder-in A two-track movement in which the horse is evenly bent along the length of its spine away from the direction of its movement.

Shy, to Wherein a horse jumps to one side having been frightened by a real or imaginary phenomenon.

Side reins Reins used while training to help position the horse's head. They are attached at one end to the bit and at the other to the girth or roller buckled around the horse's saddle or belly.

Simple change The change of leading legs at the canter executed by bringing the horse back to the trot and asking for canter again with the other leg leading.

Skewbald Refers to the coat of a horse irregularly marked with large patches of brown and white.

Snaffle bit The simplest form of bit, and the most frequently used. It consists of a straight or jointed mouthpiece and a ring at either end for the reins.

Spread fence A fence in which the main feature is the width, rather than the height.

Spurs Small metal devices (usually blunt) worn on the rider's boot to help reinforce the leg aids.

Stable management The art of looking after one or more stable horses including all aspects of their welfare.

Stall Stabling compartment. Several stalls are usually incorporated in one building. Mainly found in large establishments, such as breeding farms.

Stock A specially designed cravat, worn as part of a formal riding outfit, usually hunting dress.

Surcingle A webbing strap which passes around a horse's back and belly and is used to keep a blanket in place. Show jumpers and event riders often buckle a surcingle around their saddle as an added precaution against the girth breaking.

Tack Comprehensive term for saddlery (q.v.). A tack room is where tack is stored.

Tail guard A piece of equipment made of leather, jute or wool, designed to completely cover the dock and protect this area of the tail. Frequently used when travelling.

Thoroughbred One of the best-known breeds, the thoroughbred, known also as the English racehorse, was bred for speed in the 17th century.

Trailer The transportation vehicle for one or two horses which is drawn behind another vehicle.

Transition The act of changing gait. A walk to a trot and a trot to a canter are known as *upward transitions*. A canter to a trot and a trot to a walk are *downward transitions*.

Travers Similar to a renvers (q.v.) except the forelegs stay on the outside track of the school while the hindlegs move on an inner track.

Treble Three fences in close alignment that have to be jumped as a combination.

Triple bar A stair-case type of fence consisting of three bars of ascending height.

Turn on the forehand A school movement performed from a halt in which the hindquarters describe a circle around the forehand, with one foreleg acting as a pivot.

Turn out, to To put a horse out in a pasture or field or turn it loose in a paddock.

Upright fence A fence which is vertical, and which tests the horse's ability to jump heights.

Vice Any one of a number of bad habits which may be learned by a horse. Unless curtailed when young, they are very hard to cure.

Volte A circle of 3m (10ft) executed at a given point in the school.

Water jump An obstacle, usually comprising a low hedge, behind which is a wide expanse of water. Used in show jumping courses.

Wisp A coiled or woven 'rope' of straw used in grooming to massage the skin and muscles and improve circulation.

Withers Point at the bottom of the neck of a horse from which a horse's height is measured.

Wither pad A small pad, made of either felt or sheepskin placed under the front of the saddle to give added protection. In a well-fitting saddle, this should not be necessary.

Yawing A horse that continually opens its mouth and stretches its head outwards and down to the ground in an attempt to evade the bit.

Yearling A colt or filly between one and two years old.

Index

Page numbers in italics refer to pictures.

A

ability, show-jumping *36, 37*
action 14
aids 62, 70, *70-1*
　artificial 88, *88-9*
　common faults *71*
　counter canter 159
　downward transitions 80
　in dressage 144
　for turns and circles 82
Andalusian horse *34*
Appaloosa *35*
appetite 58
Arabs *10*
　mare and foal *21*
artificial aids 70
athleticism, in eventing *168*

B

backing 26, *27*
backing off *127, 185*
balance
　and downhill fences 190
　and drop fences 188
　of horse 66
　lacking, uphill fence *193*
　in transitions 78
balance and rhythm, in show-
　jumping 120
balanced horse 38
bandages 56, *57*
　stable 56
　tail 56
banks *132*
bedding, straw *45*
behavior, and health 58
bend
　control of *82*
　of neck, too much *83*
bit chewing 70
bits
　and fizzy horses 86
　mouthing bit 26
　Pelham bit *113*
　pressure on *70*
　variety of 112
blankets 32, 56
　day *56*
　stable 56
Blenheim Palace, dressage
　competition *144*
boarding 32, 46
　pasture 48
　part 48

self-care 48
body protector 170, *171*
bounce fences 182, *182-3*
　downhill bounce *183*
　in gridwork 174
boxing a horse 57
braiding *52*
bran mash 55
breaking in 26, *26-7*
breast plate *170*
　racing *171*
breech birth 16
breeding 14, *14-15*
bridging the reins *105*
bridles 32. 56
　double *143*
　snaffle *142*
Burdsall, Katharine 97

C

canter 76, *76-7*
　between poles 114
　collected *134*
　common faults 77
　dressage 152, *152-3*
　　common faults *153*
　over poles *92, 93*
　three-beat movement 76, *77*
　uphill *104*
canter poles *175*
canter-trot transition *155*
　lack of preparation *155*
canter-walk transition 156
　advanced horse *157*
　novice horse *156*
center of gravity (horse) 66, 90
　over a jump *90*
changing rein, gridwork 176
Chukka Cove, Jamaica *101*
circles
　counter canter *159*
　leg-yielding *164*
　and turns 82, *82-3*
　　common faults *83*
closing down the angles (jumping) *91*
clothing
　for dressage tests 142, *142-3*
　rider 33
colic 58
　unexplained 54
collected canter 152, *153*
collected trot *149*
collected walk *146*, 146
collection, novice horse *149, 152*
colostrum 16

combination fences 98, *98-9*, 180
　assessing the distances 130
　doubles 98, *98-9*
　trebles 124, *124-5*
communication, between horse and
　rider 62, 168, *169*
competition horses, and routine 50
competitive riding 32, 108, *108-9*
　dressage 140-67
　eventing 168-99
　show-jumping 110-39
competitive training, advantages of 100
concentration, lack of *123*
conformation 14, *38*
　general riding 34
contact, loss of at the walk *73*
corner fences *177*, 180, 184, *184-5*
　common faults *185*
coughing 58
counter canter 159, *159-61*
　advanced horse *159*
　common faults *161*
covering 14, *15*, 15
crash hat 170
Crepin, Margit Otto on Corlandus
　(European Championships 1989)
　38
cross-bred horses 40
cross-breeding 36
cross-country course, planning of 168
cross-country fences 180, *180-99*
　bounce fences 182, *182-3*
　corner fences 184, *184-5*
　downhill fences 190, *190-1*
　drop fences *172, 181*, 188, *188-9*
　steps, downhill and uphill 194,
　　194-5, 196, *196-7*
　table fences 186, *186-7*
　uphill fences 192, *192-3*
　water fences 198, *198-9*
cross-country position 172, *172-3*
　common faults *173*
cross-over, foreleg *162*
crosspoles 94, *98*, 98, 116
cuts and grazes 59

D

Davidson, Bruce and
　Dr Peaches (Seoul Olympics) *198*
　on JJ Babu (Burghley Horse Trials
　　1986) *181*
day blankets 56
diagonals, the trot 74
double bridle *143*
downhill, route chosen 104

downhill fences 190, *190-1*
draw-reins 113
dress, correct *112*
dressage 140-67
　advanced and novice horses 144
　the canter 152, *152-3*
　choice of horse 38, *38-9*
　clothing and tack 142, *142-3*
　half-pass 162, *162-3*
　leg-yielding 164, *164*
　passage and piaffe 166, *166*
　riding a test 167, *167*
　training for 144, *144-5*
　training of rider 144
　transitions 154, *154-5*, 156, *156-7*
　the trot
　　medium and extended 150,
　　　150-1
　　working and collected 148,
　　　148-9
　turn on the forehand 158, *158-9*
　the walk 146, *146-7*
　walk pirouette 165, *165*
dressage arena *144*
dressage marks, interpretation of *167*
dressage tests
　clothing and tack 142, *142-3*
　　common faults *143*
　requirements of the horse 167, *167*
drop fences *172, 181*, 188, *188-9*
　into water *173*
　lack of control *189*
droppings, normal 58
dry stone walls *45*
Durand, Pierre *130*

E

Ehrens, Rob
　on Ki Or Noor (Calgary 1981) *128*
　on Olympic Sunrise (Horse of the
　　Year show 1987) *118*
Erhorn, Claus
　on Fair Lady (Burghley 1985) *190*
　on Justin Thyme (Burghley 1989)
　　199
eventing 168-99
　bounce fences 182, *182-3*
　choice of horse 40, *40-1*
　corner fences 184, *184-5*
　　common faults *185*
　cross-country fences *180*, 180, *181*
　downhill fences 190, *190-1*
　drop fences 188, *188-9*
　gridwork 174, *174-5*
　　common faults *175, 177*

improving an impetuous horse 176, *176-7*
improving a sluggish horse 178, *178-9*
safety equipment 170, *170-1*
steps
downhill 194, *194-5*
uphill 196, *196-7*
table fences 186, *186-7*
uphill fences 192, *192-3*
water fences 198, *198-9*
exercising *28, 33*, 50
on road *31*
Exmoor mare and foal *20*
extended canter 152
novice and advanced horse *152, 153*
extended trot *161*
novice and advanced 150, *151*
extended walk 146, *146, 147*

F

feathers and dragon fence *129*
feed 32
feed storage 44
feeding 50, 54-5
for fitness *54*
see also pasture
fences
anticipation of *96*
approach to *96*
combination 98, *98-9*, 122, *122-3, 137*, 124, *124-5*
cross-country 180, *180-99*
doubles 98, *98-9*, 122, *122-3, 137*
common faults *99, 122*
individual 96, *96-7*
spooky 126, *126-9*
spreads 120, *120-1*
trebles 124, *124-5*
common faults *125*
uprights 118, *118-19*
fencing 44, *45, 47*
Fernyhough, Roland *108*, 108
fetlock boots 112, *113, 171*
figure-of-eight, counter canter *159*
first aid box 32, 59
fizzy horses
in dressage *145*
improver lesson 86, *86-7*
flexion
half-pass 162
leg-yielding 164
and the walk pirouette 165
flying change 138
foal slip 12, 18, *18*

foaling 16, *16-17*
early 14
foals 12
birth of 16, *16-17*
handling of 18, *18-19*
leading 12, 22, *22*
learning to be tied 24, *24*
food, weight per day 55
foot, position of *71*
forehand
turn on 158
advanced horse *158*
weight on
the canter 77
the trot *149, 151*
forward seat 90, *91*, 172
free walk *72*, 146, *146*
Fruhmann, Thomas on Grandeur *37*

G

gates 44, *45*
opening and closing *103*
girths 112
Grackle noseband *143*
grass, and nourishment 54
grazing 48, *49*, 55
Green, Lucinda on Shannagh (Badminton 1986) *187*
grids 94, 116. *116-17*, 120
approximate distance for setting up 174
setting up *116*
gridwork 174, *174-5*
common faults *117, 175, 177*
improving an impetuous horse 176-7, *176*
improving a sluggish horse 178, *178-9*
grooming 50, *51*, 52-3, *52-3*
natural 52
and stable routine 53
grooming kit 32
Gurdon, Madelaine on The Done Thing *40*

H

half-halt
in the collected trot 148, *149*
preparation for downward transitions 80
in transitions *155*
walk pirouette 165

half-pass 162, *162-3*
advanced horse *163*
common faults *163*
novice horse *162*
halters 32
halting *81*
hand aids, for downward transitions 80
hands 62
restrictive *71, 77, 177*
sympathetic *70*
uneven *71*
Hanoverians 36
stallions *12*
harmony, of horse and rider *11*, 140
hat, show-jumping 112
hay *54*, 55
head movement
the canter 76
the walk 72
health 58, *58-9*
herd instinct *23*
Hickstead, Irish Bank (Robert Smith on April Sun) *110*
highway code 102
hill work *75, 104*
hindquarters
at the canter 76
control of *71*
turns and circles 82
eventing horses 40
jumping spreads 120
jumping uprights 118, *118*
leading with, half-pass *163*
strong, show-jumping 36, *37*
hocks
at the canter 76
eventing horses 40
flexion in 148
position in jumping spreads 120, *120*
strong, show-jumping 36
Holderness-Roddam, Jane 108, *109*
horse, communicating with rider 62
horse auctions *42*
horse dealers 42
horse, observation of 64, *65*
horse sales *43*
horse transport 33
horse/owner bond, reinforced by grooming 52
horse/rider relationship 30, *31*, 38, *39*, 65
horses
boarding 32
cost of buying and keeping 32-3
for dressage 38, *38-9*
for general riding 34-5, *34*
gregariousness of 10, *11, 14, 21*
learn by repetition 64, *65*
making a choice 28, *29*, 30

malnourished 54
need for variety *63*
ownership of 28-59
schooling of 64
for show-jumping 36, *36-7*
stabled 28, *29*, 30
understanding of *64*
where to buy 42, *42-3*
hosing down *30*
Huck, Karsten on Nepomuk 8 (Olympics 1988) *129*
human/horse relationship 18

I

Imperial Stud, New South Wales, Australia *15*
impulsion
bounce fences 182
and the canter 76
and the collected trot 148, *149*
creation of 70, *70*
in the half-pass 162
jumping doubles 98, 122
jumping individual fences 96
jumping spreads *120*
jumping uprights 118
and the medium trot 150
and the sluggish horse 178, *178-9*
in transitions 78, 154
the trot 74
turns and circles 82
uphill fences *192*, 192
for uphill steps 196
in the walk 72
water fences 198
indecision *185*
indigestion 54
insurance 32
Irish cob *34*
Irish National Stud *14*
Ishoy, Cynthia on Dynasty (Olympics 1988) *39*

J

Jacquin, Lisa on For the Moment (Paris 1987) *118*
jogging *73*
jumping position 90, *90-1*, 92
common faults *91*
weak *95*
jumping saddle 112

J

jumping position 90, *90-1*, 92
    common faults *91*
    weak *95*
jumping saddle 112

K

Kineton noseband *143*
Klimke, Reiner on Ahlerich 2 (Olympics 1988) *38*
Kursinski, Anne on Starman (Hickstead 1987) *98*

L

lactation 20
lameness 58
Larrigan-Robinson, Tanya 108, *109*
laxatives 55
leading, foals 22, *22*
leading in hand 26
leading off on the correct leg 137
leaning back 67, *75*, *81*
left behind *97*
    uphill fences *192*
leg
    acceptance of *87*
    use of *85*
leg aids *70*, *158*
leg-yielding 164, *164*
legs 62
    trotting over poles *93*
legs and feet, handling of (foals) 22
leisure riding 100-5
Leng, Virginia
    on Master Craftsman *11*, *40*
    show-jumping *91*
Lewis, Annette on Tutin, unorthodox style *111*
Linsenhoff, Annkathrin *67*
Lippizaners, mares and foals *15*
log piles *186*
long-reins 26, *27*
Longson, Tanya on Pink Fizz *41*
looking down *97*
loops *83*
    leg-yielding *164*
looseboxes 44, *46*
    American type *44*
lunging *13*, 26, *26*

M

manger, fixed *55*
mares, maternal instinct *23*
mares and foals, turning out 20, *20-1*
Martindale, Sophie on Proven Best (Badminton 1986) *94*
martingales 57, 88, *143*
    running 88, *89*, *113*, *170*
    standing 88, *89*
meconium 16
medium canter 152, *153*
medium trot, novice and advanced 150, *150*
medium walk 146, *146*, *147*
Meyers, Marie on Dimitrius (Stockholm 1989) *39*
molassed chop 55
mouth, sensitive *70*
mouthing bit 26
mucking out *31*
Mustang foals *25*

N

natural aids 70
natural obstacles 100
New Zealand rugs 56, *56*
nosebands
    cavesson *142*
    dropped *142*
    flash *89*, 142, *143*
    Grackle *143*
    Kineton *143*
numnah pad 112, *113*
nutrition 20

O

obedience, dressage 144
Olympic Stadium, Seoul *133*
open country, exercising across 102, *102*
over-tracking 150
overreach boots 112, *171*
owners, working and non-working, sample routines 50
oxers 120

P

pace
    at water fences 198
    controlled, in show-jumping 132, *135*, *137*

pacing out distances 130, *130*, *175*
paddocks 44, *45*
parallel bars 120, *135*, *139*
passage 166, *166*
pasture 54
    board 48
Pelham bit 113
Phillips, Mark, Badminton Horse Trials *169*
piaffe 166, *166*
placenta 16
planks 118
pole distances 92
pole work 92, *92-3*
    for show-jumping 114, *114-15*
poles 118, 120
    leading to a small jump 94, *94*
        common faults *95*
    setting up for show-jumping *114*
ponies
    Exmoor mare and foal *20*
    Rocky Mountain *13*
    Welsh pony foal *19*
pony blood, in eventing horses *40*
position, correct *67*
practice courses 132
pregnancy 14, 16
protective boots 56, 112, *113*, *143*, *170*, *170*, *171*
protective headgear 102
Puissance wall *129*
pulse 58

R

racehorses, early foals 14
rasping, of teeth 32
rearing up *87*
reins
    for breaking in 26, *27*
    bridging *105*
    long *86*
    loose *75*
    poor contact, bounce fence *183*
    rubber-covered *170*
    schooling 57
resistance
    dressage canter *153*
    the trot *149*
respiration rate 58
rhythm
    and the canter 76
    development of 92
    in the walk 72
rider
    classic position 66

communicating with the horse 62
    position of 66, *66*, *68-9*
        common faults *67*, *69*
    positional faults 84, *84*
riding activities *33*
riding a course 132, *132-9*
    flying change 138
    leading off on the correct leg 137
riding, general, type of horse for 34, *34-5*
riding schools, part-board 48, *49*
riding techniques 64-99
rising, to the trot 74
rising trot, correct and incorrect 148, *148*
roadwork 31, 102, *102*
Robert, Michel, on Pequignet Lafayette *37*, *120*
Rocky Mountain pony *13*
Rocky Mountains, trail riding *100*
roller, fitting of 26
rolling, reasons for 52
roughage 54-5
rugs 56
    New Zealand 56
    turn-out 56
running martingale 88, *89*, *113*, *170*
running out *125*
rushing, at fences *175*

S

saddle sores *58*
Saddlebred horse *35*
saddles 26, 32
    for dressage 142
    dressage *143*
    regular *170*
    second-hand 56
safety
    in equestrian sports 112
    equipment 170, *170-1*
St Moritz, riding in the snow *101*
schooling 50, *63*
    of fizzy horses 86
    over single fences, sluggish horses 178
seat 62
    forward
        cross-country *172*
        jumping 90, *91*
    good 66
    independent 66, 70
    too forward 86
self-carriage 140
    advanced horse 144
serpentines *83*
shoeing 32

show-jumping 110-39
   choice of horse 36, *36-7*
   combination fences
      doubles 122, *122-3*
      trebles 124, *124-5*
   correct equipment 112, *112-13*
   gridwork 116, *116-17*
   planning a round *131*
   pole work 114, *114-15*
   riding a course 132, *132-9*
   spooky fences 126, *126-9*
   spreads 120, *120-1*
   training a novice *133*
   uprights 118, *118-19*
   walking the course 130, *130-1*
showing, and routine 51
side-reins 26, *27*
sitting, to the trot 74
sitting crooked 69
Skelton, Nick 97, *130*
sluggish horses
   gridwork 178, *178-9*
   improver lesson 84, *84-5*
   table fences 186, *187*
Smith, Robert on April Sun
   (Hickstead) 110
snaffle bridle 112, 142, *170*
snow, riding in *101*
soundness 14
speed and direction, changes in 132
spooky fences 126, *126-9*
   common faults *127*
   correct approach 126
spray, problem in jumping water *199*
spreads 120, *120-1*
   common faults *121*
   correct shape 120, *121*
spurs 62, 88, 142
   correctly and wrongly fitted *88*
stable blankets 56
stable blocks, modern 46, *47*
stable routine 50, *51*
   grooming *51*, 52-3, *52-3*
stable yard, cleaning up *51*
stabling
   at home 44, *44-5*
   boarding 46, *46-7*
   part-board 48, *48-9*
stallions
   choice of 14
   Hanoverian *12*
stalls 44
   indoor *48*
standing martingale 88, *89*
standing off *117*
   uphill fence *192*
   uprights *119*
steep slopes 100, *191*

steps
   downhill 194, *194-5*
   uphill 196, *196-7*
stiffness 67, *73, 77*
stirrup iron *71*
stirrup leathers
   position of *68*
   shortened 90, *91*
stride
   between elements 130
   bouncy, uphill fences 192
   collected *118*
   and gridwork 116
   lengthening and shortening 114, *115,*
      118
   seeing the stride *115*, 120
suckling 16, *17*
sugar beet pulp 55
surcingle *170*

T

table fences *169*, 180, 186, *186-7*
   sluggish/impetuous horses 186, *186,*
      187
tack
   and clothing 56-7
   comfort of 57
   for dressage tests 142, *142-3*
tack room 44, 57
tail bandages 56
taking off too early *121*
temperament 14
   for dressage 38
   of the eventing horse 40
   of horse and rider 34
temperature 58
tendon boots 112, *113*
Theodorescu, Monica on Ganimedes
   (European Championships 1989)
   140
thoroughbred horses
   and eventing 40
   feed requirement after foaling 20
tipping forward 67, *81*
Todd, Mark on Charisma *41*
tracking up 82
traffic, and horses 102
trail riding *32, 100,* 100, 102, *102-3,*
   104, *104-5*
training 65
transitions 84, 154, *154-5*, 156, *156-7*
   downward 80, *80*
      common faults *81*
      preparation and completion *80*
   upward 78, *78*

   common faults *78*
trial period 42
triple bars 120
trot
   extended *161*
   medium and extended 150, *150-1*
      common faults *151*
   technique 74, *74-5*
      common faults *75*
      a two-beat pace 74, *74*
   working and collected 148, *148-9*
      common faults *149*
trot-canter transition *78*, 155
   common faults *79*
trot-walk transition 155
   bad preparation *155*
trotting
   in gridwork 116
   over poles *92, 93*
   uphill *75*
Tucker, Angela on Charleston V,
   uphill steps *196*
turn on the forehand *see* forehand,
   turn on
turns
   and circles 82, *82-3*
      common faults *83*
   tight 132
tying up, foals 24, *24*

U

underblankets 56
uphill 104, *104*
uphill fences 192, *192-3*
   common faults 193
uphill trot *75*
uprights 118, *118-19, 134, 139*
   common faults *119*
   take off position *119*
US team, World Championships
   (Aachen 1986) *112*

V

veterinary bills 33
veterinary check, when buying a horse
   42, *43*
veterinary surgeon 58, *59*
voice 62
   importance of to foals 22
   use of 70

W

walk pirouette 165, *165*
walk, the
   dressage 146, *146-7*
   technique 72, *72-3*
      common faults *73*
      four-beat pace *73*
walk-trot transition 78, *154*
   common faults *79*
   lack of preparation *154*
walking the course 130, *130-1*
walls 118
   Puissance *129*
washing down *52*
water, clean 55
water fences 198, *198-9, 128*
water jumps 180
water tray *134, 136*
   jumping off *126*
weaning methods 25
Welsh ponies, foal *19*
whips 62, 142
   jumping and schooling *89*
   use of 88, *88*
Whitaker, John *130*
   on Next Milton (European
      Championships 1989) *36, 111*
Whitaker, Michael *130*
   on Next Monsanta (Calgary 1989) *37*
wild horses, instincts of 10
Wilding Davies, David and Crusader
   (Badminton Horse Trials 1989) *176*
Williams, Ruth and Conspirator, drop
   fence *181*
working canter 152
working livery 48
working trot *148, 148*